Applause for
My Story Continues: From Neighborhood to Junior High School

A book of Dr. Ed's stories to add to your collection …

"By far the best work Ed has done. This is a book for all age groups …
stories that will help young and old understand what is behind the road to
success. Those who are older will appreciate Dr. Ed's stories because some
parts touch on everyone's experiences. It's about respect and education."

– Mike Montigny, Author

"Reminiscent of television's *The Wonder Years, From Neighborhood to Junior
High School* conjures up laugh-out-loud memories of relatives, neighbors,
shopkeepers and school personnel. Ed's book is a fun romp through Italian
childhood in an easier era."

– Colleen Kelly Mellor, Author and Columnist

"Anyone who has had summer vacation at the beach, a favorite teacher, or a
first crush, will love Dr. Ed's latest. His vivid, descriptive writing sweeps you
back to his childhood and awakens fond memories of your own. You will
recall the wonderful feeling of hot summer days and misty, cool evenings at
the shore.
      Smell the Noxzema cream and Citronella oil in the summer. Listen in
his junior high classroom in the fall. My generation will remember and
reminisce; younger generations will learn what it was like "back in the day."
A wonderful, light-hearted read!"

– Tom DeNucci, M.D., Writer

"After his serious professional career, now in *My Story Continues: From
Neighborhood to Junior High School,* Ed Iannuccilli writes nostalgically and
with humor of youthful episodes that reveal the man as a boy. It is an
interesting book rich in local color."

– Elizabeth A. Salzillo, Author

ALSO BY ED IANNUCCILLI

Growing Up Italian: Grandfather's Fig Tree and Other Stories

What Ever Happened to Sunday Dinner?

I'm here!

MY STORY CONTINUES:

from NEIGHBORHOOD to JUNIOR HIGH SCHOOL

ED IANNUCCILLI

For permission requests, write to the publisher, addressed
"Attention: Permissions Coordinator," at the address below.

CreateSpace
4900 LaCross Road
North Charleston, SC 29406
USA Ordering Information: Amazon Books

Quantity sales:
Special discounts are available on quantity purchases by corporations,
associations, and others. For details, contact the publisher at the address above.

Orders by U.S. trade bookstores and wholesalers:
Please contact Big Distribution:
Tel: (800) 800-8000; Fax: (800) 800-8001
or visit www.bigbooks.com.

Printed in the United States of America
Set in Garamond Classico

www.amazonbooks.com

ISBN 978-0-692-95484-3

Designed by Randy Walters
randywalters.com

DEDICATION

To my Family, Neighbors, Teachers and Lifelong Friends

CONTENTS

INTRODUCTION

I define myself with stories that relive the fun of my early years in a small, easily-managed world. It was like a club, one I could enter and leave as I wished. When I entered that club, I was comfortable. When I left, I wanted to re-enter.

Save for the memories, there is little left of the neighborhood and the weave of families that helped to shape my life. These essays are a sentimental glance to a time that made me what I was to become.

What I write of stores, streets, schools, houses, sidewalks, streetcars, telephone poles, gardens, neighbors and friends is in a small world on a few city blocks.

The neighborhood was a savory stew of people; immigrants, their children and their children's children. There was not a face or a voice I did not recognize. Most were Italian or Irish. While my grandmother was singing *Vicin 'u Mare*, my mother was singing *Fascination*, I was singing *Earth Angel* and someone else was singing *Danny Boy*. We not only melted into America, we melted into each other.

Why this format of short stories rather than an overarching memoir? Because that is how I remember them; in snippets and scraps of nostalgia. The more I write, the more these anecdotes pop up. They recreate the extended neighborhood of family, relatives, friends, churches, games and cultures – a look to the past through a kaleidoscopic lens.

Unlike the usual memoir, I have no glaring announcements, no scandals and not much family dysfunction. It is a quiet, nurturing, predictable, fun-filled childhood.

One other thing. Conversations are fictional of course, but I recreate them either to make a point or to embellish a story. I cannot swear to the exact words, but they are true in essence.

Trust me.

Your Author, Hard at Work

CHAPTER ONE

ELEMENTARY SCHOOL

My Elementary School

I walked to school three times a day, past the governor's, teacher's and singer's homes, past the bakery, the flower shop, then the funeral parlor and the variety store. Hidden from the street, the Academy Avenue School was bunkered by a high, dark, cranberry-colored stone wall.

Atop the wall was a black wrought iron fence. Homes bordered one side while the other side reached along the Cambridge Street hill. The rear of the school, deep in a well and bordered by the same wall and fence, was one of the top three neighborhood stickball arenas.

The front yard was a tarred, open area where we waited in line for the bell at the start of school, upon return from lunch, after recess or a fire drill. During recess, I traded or pitched cards to the wall alongside the outdoor staircase; a 'stander' requiring the throw of three more cards to knock it down. I pitched pennies. I played tag, touch football and dodge ball or just huddled with friends. One day, terrified and frozen, I paid Gilbert and Robert a nickel for protection.

A huge structure of two stories, Academy Avenue School had wooden stairways and creaky, uneven wooden floors. Its globes hung from the high ceilings. Next to one of the tall windows stood a stick with a hook used to open and close them.

At Academy, I experienced the dentist and the Schick test.

"I have a dentist," I pleaded with Miss Howard, our principal. "He's my cousin."

"It does not matter. It is the rule. You HAVE to see the school dentist."

Steve and Bob told me that the dentist stuck in a big needle and screwed it to the bone. "You can hear it grind."

"Thanks, guys."

I shuffled at snail's pace and stood at the door. "Get on in, Edward," I heard Mrs. Dooley (we heard that she had lost her husband in the war), my teacher, say. "He is waiting for you."

With the speed of a turtle, I turned the handle using the tips of my fingers. He stood before me, a tall person in a white tunic "Come in, come in, son. Have a seat." He pointed to a gigantic chair with a black seat, black back, black headrest and a black pad too far away for my little legs.

I climbed up. He opened a folder. "Hello, Edward." He had a ruddy face, wore wire-rimmed glasses and was too somber. I eyed the clock, its sticky hands ticking in molasses.

"Just a check-up. That's all. Don't worry." He must have been aware of my wide eyes, quaking legs and tight jaw muscles.

Through taut, thin, inflexible lips I muttered, "I, uh, uh, dunt hev iny cvities. My cousn, Dotta Lapolla, tik kere of em, uh, list smmr. Duh ya no im?"

"No, I do not, son. Open. From nowhere, he swiveled a flat, white stand that took its place just over my knees, imprisoning me. On the stand was an assortment of weapons ... a huge needle, a screwdriver, hammer, wrench, hand drill, oil can, like the stuff at Dad's workbench. A doily did not help. He accidently knocked a drill hanging on an arm of apprehension over me. I looked up. He tapped it away and swung it out of view.

"Open." His huge hand was holding some sort of curled metal item like Mom's knitting needle. His fingers were baseball bats.

"What was lockjaw?" I wondered, while glancing at the clock and out the tall window at cars passing on Academy Avenue. The hum of the traffic and the steady tick of the clock calmed me. "Gee," I thought, "This school is high. I can see over the wall and the fence and, over there, on Cambridge, is Aunt Mary's house. And uncle's store is around the corner."

"Open." Back to reality. I opened a bit. In a flash, he jammed a rubber block to one side. I was frozen, open. He tapped, tinkled and scratched each tooth as if he were playing a xylophone. It was an eternity before he said, "All set. No cavities. Some fillings. Good luck."

"That's it? I'm done!" The clock ticked with a bang.

"Yes, Edward. Good luck." (Thank you, Doctor Lapolla.) I jumped off the chair, spun and ran at top speed out the door and into the corridor where I met Steve and Bob.

"What happened?" they cried.

"What happened?! Are you kiddin! He has a huge needle. He grinds it in jes as you said. That's what happened. The drill. The sound of the drill. OmaGod." A pasty pall disabled them. With a thin smile, I cradled my jaw in my hands and whisked away. "See ya."

The Schick Test

"Children, you will have to have the Schick test to see if you have diphtheria. Take this paper home to have it signed by your parent." For an instant, I thought I might talk Dad out of signing. I didn't. He would know it was the right thing, so I submitted.

We lined up for the school nurse; the nice one who caressed our scrapes and swabbed our poison ivy. She was sitting at a table covered with a white tablecloth and harboring a bunch of needles, a bottle of alcohol and a box of cotton swabs. Not the tools of a dentist, but frightening nonetheless. The room smelled of alcohol. Kids shifted from one leg to another as they stood in line. Four ahead of me, now three, now two, now one and now my turn. She rubbed my skin with the cotton and alcohol and said, "This will just pinch."

"Yeah, right," I thought. I looked back. "No whimpering," I muttered into my collar.

She cradled my forearm and raised the tiny needle between two fingers. I flinched at the pinch. She was right. I walked away standing tall, holding my arm like Superman as I approached my friends to ask, "OK, guys, what happens now?"

They said, "Well, we heard that if the spot where she stuck the needle does not get red and bumpy, then they send you to the doctor who has to give ya a big shot in the top of your arm. He uses a big, big, needle. Look, there's Bessie. She must have just gotten the big needle." Bessie hustled by holding her arm, a tear in her eye. I'm not sure why I asked these guys anything.

"Bessie, what happened? Hey, Bessie." She hurried by, head down, mute.

"Uh oh," I thought.

I went home and stared at my arm. "Edward, stop looking at your arm. You'll be fine." On the third day, I went to the nurse for a check. "No redness, no bump, Edward. You're fine."

Academy's nearby stores were part of our education. Abe's Variety was across the street. There we purchased penny candy, plied the gumball machine and played the pinball machine. There was action outside with kids playing chestnuts winging for kingers, the Filipino Duncan Yo-Yo man with his knapsack full of tricks and a knife to carve a scene on your Yo-Yo.

Down the street on Putnam was Madeline, the solemn lady in her variety store, the one with the pickle barrel. For a nickel, Madeline made one of her rare moves, scraped off her seat to the aromatic barrel, rolled up her sleeve, reached in and pulled out the perfect, puckering prize: the jaw-aching pickle.

For three years, Academy Avenue School was a stop along the journey between the bricks of Putnam Street and George J. West Schools. I loved the teachers. I loved the neighborhood and the walks to those schools.

"In September, I'll be in junior high," I thought. "For now, I'll just enjoy the summer."

Academy will soon be history. George J. West was on the horizon.

Before that, here are some Academy Avenue School stories.

We Three Kings. My Singing Debut

It was Christmas and time for our annual play; the one that readied us for the holiday season of 1951. Christmas decorations of snowflakes, dancing snowmen holding hands and interlocking rings of red and green splashed across the classroom windows. It was the memorable year of my singing debut that started with Mrs. Dooley.

"Edward, how would you like to be one of the three kings in the story of the Christ Child?"

"A king?"

"Yes, and you can sing the part of one of the kings."

"Where."

"On the stage." My only other time on that stage was when I gave a book report in front of the entire school. I knew stage fright.

"In front of the whole school?" Uh oh, here we go again.

"Why, yes, of course."

"No way. Really, no kiddin', no way. Sing? I cannot sing. I never sing."

"Well there's no time like now to start." That didn't work.

"On the stage? In front of the whole school? All those kids, the teachers and the principal? Miss Howard does not like me. She relieved me of my duties as a crossing guard because I dragged the Stop/Go flag on the ground." That didn't work either.

"Sure. It will be a great experience." She gazed at me with her warm blue eyes.

"I'm too small. So is my voice."

"Don't worry. They'll hear you." She beamed. That didn't work.

Having attended catechism class, I knew the story of the kings bearing gifts and following the star, even though I could never remember or pronounce their names or their gifts. I shifted my plea. "I'm too nervous." That didn't work.

"Oh, forget it, Edward. You will be fine. You'll sing the chorus with Roland and Richard and then do your solo."

"A solo!" Oh, no. "Uhhh. OK."

"Good."

I was doomed to singing purgatory where the notes fly to snickering kids; the worst place imaginable. What would my friends think? And the girls? I'm ruined.

We practiced during the day. With no audience and in the empty auditorium, I was fine. My voice sounded pretty good as the notes bounced from floor to ceiling to walls. The day of the show was different. My knees were knocking. As I looked at my Dick Tracy watch wondering when it would be over, I noticed my hand shaking.

"You will meet in the classroom near the auditorium one hour before to put on your costumes." Mrs. Dooley walked toward me carrying colored sheets of reds, blues and purples in one hand and in the other, she dangled three high hats.

"Here, Edward. Put this on your head. And wrap this around your shoulders." I placed the tall, yellow and gold cardboard hat with peaks and two gold tails that draped down my back on my head. I was a King, standing tall until I shouldered the purple robe. It was too long, and I tripped, feeling like Dopey in the Seven Dwarfs. Mrs. Dooley rolled it up to my ankles.

"Oh and here. Don't forget these." She handed me a long stick and a box wrapped in gold foil. "The stick is your king's staff. In the box is your gift for the Baby Jesus, a golden chest filled with frankincense." I shook the box. No sound. Frankincense must be really light.

We strolled into the auditorium. I looked at the stage, higher now that every eye would be on me. I looked out the cloudy plate glass windows high above. There were curved rims of ice on each of their corners. The sky was a gray-white. "Snow is coming," I thought. "We'll have a white Christmas." I wanted a Flexible Flyer, so I started to dream of the snow-covered hill near the golf course. I was startled back to reality by the clangorous vibration of the bell.

The doors blew open and a booming buzz buckled the room as the kids tromped in. With the excitement of the season building, they bumped into the rows, smashed their folding seats and plopped down with excitement bordering on frenzy. The decibel count was out of sight.

The show was the last thing before Christmas break. Those students had skates, sleds and sugarplums dancing in their heads.

As Miss Howard raised her hand, the roar dipped to a rumble and then silence. Scowling teachers tapped kids on the shoulders.

"Stay here a moment," said Mrs. Dooley. "Near the steps. I'll let you know when to come up." To the rear of the stage was the nativity scene where my friend Joseph, who was playing Joseph, was dressed in a plain brown cloth. He had an enviable silent part. Joanie, dressed in blue, was Mary. She cradled a doll wrapped in white. She too was silent. Surrounded by kids in cow and sheep costumes, all they had to do was to remain motionless and look at the Baby Jesus. Lucky them.

"OK, OK, get up there. Kings to the front. Sheep and cows to the rear." I approached the front of the stage with the other kings, Roland and Richard, who were much bigger. A note from the piano rang and the teacher whispered. "OK, boys. Start."

We angled toward the Baby Jesus and started to sing, Roland's voice booming over the masses and covering me.

A whisper. "Edward, hold up your gift." Oh yes, the gift. I tucked the staff under my arm. It nearly fell, but with the skill of a circus acrobat, I caught it. The piano teacher raised her hand, held it a moment and then flicked her wrist. We started,

We three kings of orient are,
Bearing gifts we traverse afar

Field and fountain,
Moor and mountain,
Following yonder star.

That was easy, but I still had my solo. Roland did his. Richard did his. Mine came too soon. The cloak shielded my knocking knees.

Wait. Something changed! I could not believe it. I was no longer nervous or yearning for home. My knees were doing something else under that King's garment. They were swinging to the beat of the piano … we three kings da, da, da, da, dahhhh…! No longer Edward, I became Melchior, confident, capable. Da, da, da, da, da, da, da, da …

I looked at the globes pouring light on the assembly. I noticed the flaking ceiling, but I wasn't going to tell Miss Howard. "Your turn." Mrs. Dooley, out of view, whispered from below the stage. Teachers stood at attention in the back of the room with their arms folded. "Sing over the crowd to the back of the auditorium." Stretching to my toes, rising to the direction of the piano, knees swinging, feeling like a king, thinking about vacation, with a deep gasp and rumbling in my chest, I burst out … my solo …

Born a King on Bethlehem's plain,

The notes flowed like honey from my oval shaped mouth. I was regal, a star, floating over the crowd like an angel, err, rather a King. For the moment, I was THE King.

Gold I bring to crown Him again … da, da, da, da, da, da, da, da …

I held up a gold colored box of Frankincense.

King forever, ceasing neh-eh-ver

I sang with confidence. My crown wobbled.

Over us all to reign.

Another deep breath and it was over. I was frozen, content, pleased. I heard a whisper. "The gift Edward, the gift!"

Oh yeah, the gift. I turned, walked to the manger, lifted my hands and with a slight flex, lowered the gift ever so slowly, placing it in front of the Baby Jesus. I glanced over my shoulder. Mrs. Dooley was smiling. I scanned the other side to see Miss Howard, smiling. The crowd had to love it.

We sang the chorus again.

O star of wonder, star of night,
Star with royal beauty bright.
Westward leading, still proceeding,
Guide us to thy perfect light, la, ight …

We were done. My majestic, regal role was over.

The students sang "We Wish you a Merry Christmas." Santa rang a bell. A war whoop sprung from the crowd.

I bolted down the stairs, ran to the dressing room, tossed the crown, gift and sheet into the pile, ran out of the room, bounded down the stairs and out to a crystal clear sky. Vacation had started. Christmas was in the air.

Guide me home, O star of wonder and light … da, da, da, da, daaaa.

Unforgettable Gym Teachers. This One is Lud

W hy is it that gym teachers are high on the list of lasting impressions? What made them different and memorable? Mr. DG was one of those for me. He was at Academy Avenue School fixture. As I recollect those years, I realize that he made a difference.

I loved his class. Initially, he frightened me with his gruff, threatening, deep voice. He rarely smiled and never laughed. As I remember, his hair and his eyes were black. He wore black pants, polished, black gym shoes with black laces and a crisp, blue shirt. Quite fit himself, I thought he could have been a boxing champ.

His classes were in a basement room with a low ceiling supported by thick, maroon, hard metal poles. While we waited in line to do our exercises, he let us talk in low voices. That was not allowed in other classes.

He separated the class according to size. I was one of the small ones. "OK, you, over here, you there, you, you, you … there." On it went until we were organized, large kids across from small kids, ready to go, but not at each other.

We lined up to do somersaults, handstands, headstands and cartwheels. Firm canvas mats were interspersed among the poles. Oddly, the smell of mats, leather and a bit of sweat were not unpleasant to me.

With the handstand, we balanced first on our hands, then knees on our elbows with head and feet off the mat. I held it. From there, I did a head-stand by touching my forehead to the canvas and holding my body vertical with toes pointed to the ceiling. I loved it when the bigger kids could not get their thick knees on their elbows. I looked to Mr. DG. A smile perhaps?

He taught another exercise that I did for years; the horizontal stretch using one of the poles. Hands and arms around the pole, left elbow on hip and then a layout stretch, legs together, parallel and suspended above the floor. When I sat down, I looked at Mr. DG. I could do the stuff he wanted with little difficulty. He built my confidence by softly saying, "Nice job."

If he was so tough, why did I like him?

I loved his class because I knew what he expected, and I was able to do it. He never failed to acknowledge when I did well. "Good job, Iannuccilli." Not Edward. Rather Iannuccilli. I liked that.

Following the three years at Academy, I went to junior high school but never really forgot Mr. DG. I met him again in high school. He was the gym teacher for the two schools that shared the City Gym; Classical and Central. I learned that he was an all-state football player for Central. No surprise. Mr. DG remembered me. "Hey, Iannuccilli. At Classical now, eh?"

"Yes, Mr. DG."

"Good luck. It's a good place." He was mellow. Not less demanding; just mellow.

"Thank you."

Years later, we met again. He became my patient. Now I was his coach. A terrible illness reversed our roles. He needed help. It was difficult for me to see him that way; remembering him as the person in charge, the one who controlled. In caring for him, I tried to distract him from his infirmity, from his resolution that he was no longer in charge, that he was now weak, diminishing rapidly. It was difficult for both of us.

"You know, Mr. DG, I still do those exercises you taught me so many years ago."

He beamed a warm smile and voiced feebly, "Doctor, you can call me Lud. Keep up the exercises." I learned that his name, Lud, was wonderfully Italian; Ludovico, of ducal heritage.

I revisited why I liked him so much in those elementary days. He taught me discipline. With a nod and a turn of the corners of his mouth, he taught me that if I tried, I might succeed, but if not, I should be pleased with the effort. He taught me structure. I liked that. Most of all, he taught us all that no matter the size, we were all equal.

Mr. DG, Lud, was one who helped to set the patterns for the person I became. He was a treasured teacher who made a difference.

The Pinball Machine

With little to do the week before we went to our beach house, I played the pinball machine at Abe's, the local variety store across the street from the elementary school, between the flower shop and a dry goods store.

Abe was a small, pale, balding man with a gray stubble of beard. As I remember, he wore glasses with clear frames. He could easily have been a bookkeeper like Dickens' Scrooge or Bartleby the Scrivener. He wore suspenders like those of the old Italian men.

Abe went home for lunch in the summer. He reopened at one o'clock. I was his first customer. Head down, tired, melancholy, Abe murmured, unlocked the door, groaned it open and did not look up until he gave me my Chunky and my change. I loved the Chunky, a dense pyramid square of chocolate loaded with nuts, cashews and raisins.

Abe stored his candy behind a smoky, milk glass container. On school days, he seemed annoyed. Kids leaned against the glass. He shifted his feet, looked up at the ceiling, shrugged and blurted, "Get back, get back, you kids." He pawed the candy with three fingers of his right hand, picking off pieces when the kids pointed, then dropping them into a small white bag which he held in his left hand. When flustered, he muttered a hushed "Hurry up kid. C'mon."

This day he was not flustered because he knew what I wanted, and there were no clamoring kids. I gave him my quarter. He returned the Chunky and four nickles. I strolled across the oily, buckled floor to a machine cornered against the window. I stood at the machine, draped my hands over the sides, slid them up and down along the smooth, worn wood and caressed the flippers' buttons. Near the plunger, I spotted a little door with a lock, behind which were the nickles gobbled by the machine.

I reached into my pocket, fondled my nickels and pulled one, holding it next to the slot. The painted glass at the opposite end was the command center that displayed points, flashed lights and made captivating noises … knuck, knuck, knuck … for bonus games.

Nickel in … blurt, bang, bang, ring, ring-a-ding, ding, bop, blurp, a sound deep within of silver balls dropping … one, two, three, four, five. I pushed the plunger and into the slot arose the first smooth, silver beauty.

I pulled the springer back, held it a moment and let go, shooting the ball up the right side to the uppermost curve where it speedily straddled back and forth across the bend along the top, finally stopped and made its descent. I rose to my toes. The orb zigged and zagged, picking up speed as it moved down the table. It rattled down into slots … bing, bing, bing … and popped out … ka-ching … as if shot from a cannon, ricocheted between bumpers and poles that lit up when hit, racked up points along its way and hit the sides while heading toward my flippers.

As the ball hit its targets, flashes of electrical energy, lights, chimes, bells and buzzers screamed. More noise meant more points and more points meant more knucks! Pop bumpers, dead bumpers, slingshots, kick out holes, targets, roto targets, bells and animations scored my journey.

At the bottom, dead in the middle, was the dreaded drain, the sinkhole oblivion where eventually all balls were lost. The flippers, the only protection from the hole, were too far apart.

Trying to keep the ball from our arch enemy, gravity, I wielded them; first the right, then the left, then both, shooting a ball back into play all the way to the top, but the dreaded sink hole was too big. Ahhhh, but there was more to do before finality – one more chance. Rock the machine. Rock it when Abe was not watching. Rock it for control. Rock it to save the ball and me. However, there was the dreaded tilt, a dastardly device designed to control the game.

Robert was best at jiggling the machine. With his tongue out and the body language of a contortionist, he shook, coddled and caressed the contraption so that he could stand it almost upright without tilting the game. Me? It seemed that all I had to do was take a deep breath, and I was a tilt goner. OK. It was cheating anyway.

The machine ate my nickels rather quickly, and I was on my way back home. Sure, I had a few free games now and then, but not enough to occupy the entire afternoon. As I walked along, I thought, "Except for the Chunky, I wasted my money. I'm not doing that again."

Today, I think about the game. Pinball is like life with its wins and losses, sensitive unreliable flippers, things at the top, then at the bottom and a big hole to summon failure. There were no replays. The tilt was sensitive, and you lost if you were not careful.

Losing was so fast, so final, and I hated it. Was the trip to Abe's, the Chunky and the challenge worth it? You bet.

CHAPTER TWO

GROWING UP STORIES

My First Time Alone on a Pony

After years of being led counterclockwise around the dusty oval by a speechless, sad, depressed woman alone in her corral, I felt it was time. It was time for me to ride a pony by myself. After all, I was ten. On an occasional Sunday, we visited Roger Williams Park, an oasis of fun, relaxation and recreation in the center of the city. We visited the animals, went on rides, attended a concert at the band shell or sometimes just rode around in Dad's car. In the winter, we went sledding on the hills and ice-skating on Polo Lake.

The rides were fun; a carousel, boats, motorized bumper cars and the ponies. I rode the gas car. The attendant, a dirty red handkerchief tucked in the back pocket of his greasy dungarees, gave it a kick-start by jamming a plunger at the rear of the car. A puff of black smoke and off I went on the short track, twice, steering wheel in hand, hitting wooden bumpers that guided me until I reached the end where the same attendant stopped the car. Confined and controlled at a slow and predictable speed, I could not, and did not, fail.

Nearby were the ponies. The smell of hay and manure reminded me of cowboy movies. The muddy van that transported the ponies was beyond the corral. On previous rides, the woman who drove the van held the reins of my pony and walked me around the corral. Twice. It was boring. "Hi,

Edward, Hi," Mom yipped as I made the turn without looking up for fear someone might spot me.

Oh, the boredom of riding a droopy pony led by a weary lady in scruffy cowboy boots, a plaid wool shirt, a sweat-stained ten gallon hat, a bulky flannel jacket open at the bottom and worn dungarees held by a big-buckled belt. This Sunday I thought, "This is the day I ride the pony, alone."

I was dressed in my best clothes, the ones Mom prescribed; nice pants, Buster Brown shoes, a jacket and shirt buttoned to the top. "Dad, I'm tired of the lady and the slow pony. I want to ride alone. Can you tell her?"

"Are you sure, Edward?"

"Yes. I know I can. Please."

"OK. We'll try it this one time, but be careful."

"Are you sure, Peter?" Mom was lurking.

"Why not. He's old enough."

'I can do it, Mom.'

"No, Peter."

Dad looked at mom, then at me. "Go ahead, Edward. Give it a try." He bought five tickets and walked toward the lady. "When it is his turn, let him go alone." Thumbs in her belt, muddy boots spread wide, she nodded.

I stood in line with a sense of power over the other kids. I reached the front and handed that lady my ticket. "I'm riding alone, today," I beamed. I wished I had cowboy boots and a ten gallon cowboy hat.

She droned, "Yep. Alone. OK. That one." She pointed to a jet black pony almost as big as a horse. He was biting on his bit and foaming. The pervasive smell of manure and leather stirred my interest.

"What's his name?"

"What?" She flicked her chin up.

"What's the pony's name?"

"Lightning."

No more talking. She had enough. Lightning shook his head. Foam sprinkled the air, nearly hitting me. I moved closer. I stroked his head but pulled back in a start when he jolted and dug his front hooves deeper into the wet dirt. Dad clenched his cigar between his front teeth. Mom walked away.

The lady took the reins off the post. Hands on hips, she woofed, "Git up on 'er." I paced. "C'mon, kid. Put yer foot in." I put my left Buster Brown in the stirrup. With her large hand on my butt, she gave me a boost. I whisked my right over the saddle and put the other Buster Brown in the other stirrup. The pony jerked, his ears back and twitching. "Ah ya on 'im?" she droned. I held the saddle horn with both hands.

"What?"

"Ah … ya … on … 'im? Dern it. Dunt yer unnerstan inglish? Grab the rins."

She hit his rump and that did it! I never had a chance to say "Gimmee a minute, willya." The sucker took off, his hooves throwing dirt high into the air. I never did grab the reins. Lightning became a beast, a derby winner, dust flying everywhere. He was raw power that I could not control. I choked the horn of the saddle.

He hugged the rail. I was bumping around in the saddle like sliding down stairs on my butt. In an instant, he slammed into the rail. My shoe came out of the right stirrup and my foot was bouncing to the tempo of the gallop. It swung completely around and was on the same side as my left which was still in the stirrup. Sitting sidesaddle, now I lost the horn. I grabbed his mane and held tight.

"Peter, Peter," I heard Mom scream. Something was driving this beast? A smell? Food? Me?

A final kick and I was airborne, thrown to the other side of the fence. Thump. From the ground, I watched the pony stop at the next bend, as calm as a grazing cow. I jumped up. My head hurt. My chin hurt. My shoulder hurt. Dazed and bewildered, I looked around trying to figure out where I was. After a second whirl, I spotted Dad.

I vaulted the fence and ran across the track. I scaled the second fence. Dad was there. He always was.

"Too much horse for you, Edward. Maybe too soon." I took the four tickets out of my pocket and gave them to Dad. I turned around hoping Mom wouldn't do something stupid like hug me.

"No he wasn't! No." Sniff. "*She* never gave me a chance to get set in the saddle. It was her fault." I put my hands in my pockets and walked head down to the car.

"Gess 'e wuz jes not reiddy ta ride taday," that person groaned to Dad. "Ya wint me ta da somfin wit da udder tickets?"

"Yeah, here. You take them," replied Dad. "Give them to another kid."

I sat in the car. The little sensation on my chin was blood which I rubbed with the back of my hand. The next week, I returned to the bumper cars.

The Crew Cut. Oops, I Mean a Rah-Rah

The door opened directly from the street into the barbershop with its small, white, diamond shaped floor tiles. It smelled of lime, alcohol, soap, talcum powder, leather and perfume. It anchored a building with two tenements above and the shoemaker's shop next door. In its own way, it was charming.

To the front were two chairs with barbers wading through hair covering the floor and the tips of their shoes. A large mirror with postcards taped to it ran the length of the wall in front of the barber chairs. To the right of the door was a row of seats, three on each side of a wobbly wooden table loaded with magazines and newspapers, some current. Two customers were in the chairs and two were waiting, comfortably sharing stories of work, baseball and families. It was summer. Two overhead fans holding globe lights wobbled, barely moving any air.

I sat in a chair and after a careful search, slipped a National Geographic off the table. "Gonna look for the naked girls, kid," Arthur the Barber was quick to quip. The guy next to me smiled. I blushed, closed the Geographic and lay it under the newspaper, grabbing a Look Magazine with one blinding pass.

Arthur the Barber was my barber ever since I left Gigi the Barber, Dad's lifelong friend. Gigi had a shop on Federal Hill, and when I was young and small, he used a seat booster that slung across the arms of the barber chair. On Saturdays, Gigi's radio was tuned to the opera.

When I went to Arthur's at the end of our street, I was older, unescorted, and no longer needed a booster seat. Arthur used a power foot pump to raise his chair. Just as the shoemaker next door wore a leather apron, Arthur wore his trademark gray tunic. He had silver hair and pinched eyes. And I don't think he liked opera.

"Next." I climbed on the steel footrest and glided into the seat. My feet dangled as I snuggled into the soft red leather rippled with cracks, lay my arms on the red leather armrests and looked out the window through the 'Barber Shop' letters. There I saw the twirling barber pole, cars passing and Abe's Variety across the street (Abe had moved from his spot near the school). The conversation may have gone something like this:

"How ya doing', Kid?" Arthur asked as he pumped the chair.

"Good, thank you."

"Howse ya Mom and Dad?"

"Good."

"Did ya get promoted?"

"Yes."

"Are ya playin' any baseball?"

"Yes."

"Did ya get any hits in the ball game?"

"Yes, two."

"Good goin'."

Barber talk over, it was time for business.

"Whatsup?" He put tissue paper around my neck, snapped open a black and white striped smock and with a flick, cinched it too tight around my neck with a large safety pin and fluffed it to the tops of my sneaks.

"Can I get a rah-rah today?" I coughed.

"Too tight."

"No," I squealed.

"Ya mean a crew cut?"

"No, a rah-rah." That's what my friends called it.

"Well I cut it down ta da scalp, ya know."

"Yes. I know."

"Does ya mother know?"

"Yes." I thought of a conversation with Mom.

"Your face is too small for a rah-rah," blurted Mom as she looked up from the newspaper.

"All the guys get them for the summer. Dan is." That endorsed it. Dan was my best friend.

"But all those beautiful curls."

"That's what I want to get rid of, Mom. It will make me a faster swimmer, no hair in my eyes, I won't sweat as much, I'll look older, and I won't have to comb it."

"OK, I guess. Your choice."

"I thought they called it a crew cut," said Dad.

"Nope. It's a rah-rah."

"Rah-rah, crew cut, go ahead. Here's the money." He gave me fifty cents.

I awoke from that conversation to Arthur's warning. "OK. Here goes."

I looked at the large mirror. Below it was a white marble counter with a bunch of things on it; tools, hand clippers, a black comb, a group of scissors, bottles with green, red and white liquids, a radio and a razor that folded into a pearl handle. There was a hook that held an electric razor. I looked in the mirror at my curly hair. If I knew then what a wistful look was, perhaps that was it.

Arthur slapped a bear's paw on my head, expecting, I guess, that I would be restless. Maybe he thought I would bolt when I saw the clippers.

He practiced a clip, stood back and with a sideways glance ran the clippers across the top as if he were cutting a lawn; right to left, front to back ... clip, clip, clip ... up the sides ... with the speed and skill of a surgeon. From the corner of my eye, I glanced at the mirror and watched the curls tumble and disappear over my shoulders, down my arms and to the floor. Arthur turned to a customer, "Did the Yankees win last night?"

I thought, "Wait, wait, Arthur. This is a rah-rah I'm getting, the biggest decision of my life, and you want to know about the Yankees?!" I stayed quiet. He had the weapons. I closed my eyes and lowered my head. Arthur snapped it up. "Take a look, kid." It seemed a long time before I opened my eyes and when I did, I was stunned. Save for short fuzz, I was bald. No curls. I noticed a scar where someone hit me with a rock. "Is it OK?"

"Uh yes, I guess."

Arthur unsnapped the pin, swirled the cape and shook it, piling more hair on the floor. He removed the tissue, crumpled it, threw it in the basket, replaced the cape but did not tighten it and snapped the pin.

"Not quite done, kid. I gotta shave yer neck."

Hanging alongside the chair was a leather strap. The only memory I had of a strap was my uncle's. He hung his in a broom closet, bringing it out to show his kids when he was angry. "If you don't behave, I'll use the strap." He never did, but he always threatened, "I'll get the strap, I'll get the strap!" as he ran to the closet, stopping short, rarely opening its door.

"What is that strap for?"

"Notta strap, son. It's a strop, a strop, a rayza strop. I use it to sharpen my rayza." He flipped open the razor with his right hand and holding the strop horizontally and slightly bowed with his left ... whoosh, whoosh, whoosh ... slid and flipped the blade along the leather with the speed of a huntsman. He did everything but blow on the razor when he was finished.

He touched it gently. "It's a little warm." The blade gleamed. With a short brush, he lathered soap in a jar, slabbed it on my neck and with ever so gentle top to bottom motions, shaved. It felt good until he applied the white liquid. "Ouch." I rubbed my neck and looked at my hand to see if there was any blood.

'Only stings for a minute, Kid."

Arthur sprinkled powder on a soft dry brush and slapped it across my face, nose and neck. Talc flew. Hair flew; much of it down my neck and shirt. On those hot days, the hair drove me crazy. I needed a bath.

"All set." He rubbed my head. A few more hairs flew. Slapping Vitalis on his hands, he rubbed it over the remaining bristles. I loved its smell.

I jumped off the chair, paid Arthur and skipped out rubbing my soft fuzz. Even though I liked it, I looked around to be sure no one saw me as I headed up the street to home. I met Dan, my best friend. He did not have a rah-rah.

"I thought you were getting your rah-rah today?"

"Nope. My mother wouldn't let me." I glared at him. "This might be a long summer," I thought.

Eighty-Six Comic Books Made Me Happy and Sad

I caught the comic book frenzy from my friends. We bought and swapped for a while, but being somewhat possessive, I stopped trading. I even stopped buying them because the eighty-six were enough to keep me occupied.

I kept them in the safest place I knew; the bottom draw of the large bureau on the other side of my bedroom, right under Dad's pristine copy of the 1938 *Providence Journal,* the one that headlined *The* Hurricane.

The books were an escape. The stories were just plain good; believable conflicts with good and bad guys, just like in the movies. I read them over and over, putting the latest at the bottom of the pile. Reading one a day, it was a while before I got back to the first, but when I did, I had a new book.

The eighty-six was a big league collection with an all-star cast: *Archie, Superman, Captain Marvel, Green Lantern, Batman, Tarzan, Plastic Man, Wonder Woman* and my favorite cowboys – Roy and Gene. I read about *Donald Duck,* his *Uncle Scrooge* and his mischievous nephews; Huey, Louie and Dewey. Nancy, Sluggo, Mary Jane, Sniffles and *Archie* were in the pile. I had a warm spot for Archie and his friends because they hung out at a soda shop that was much like the one I went to with friends after the Friday night movies. Oh yes, I loved *The Katzenjammer Kids.*

I also read the daily 'funnies' while kneeling, hands on my chin, on the linoleum floor in front of the Barstow Stove; a globe above lighting the way.

Blondie, L'il Abner, Rex Morgan, M.D. and *L'il Henry* were part of the company. The Sunday funnies, in color, were even better. *Tarzan* reappeared along with *Terry and the Pirates* and *Buzz Sawyer.*

I owned a few *Classics Illustrated; Ivanhoe, The Count of Monte Cristo* and *The Three Musketeers.* They gave me a sense that these comics were OK, literature so to speak. After all, they were classics, absolving me of the guilt of not reading "the real thing."

The comics were just plain good; good guys defeating the enemy, teenage stars, daredevils taking chances and heroes always winning. They made me feel good and happy. The sad part?

On those quiet evenings when Mom worked winding golf balls at US Rubber and Dad, Peter and I sat at the kitchen table, we seemed to have little to say. Mom was the animated one. With her gone, the only sounds were the scraping of dishes and an occasional rustling of papers – Dad when he folded the *Evening Bulletin,* Peter and I when we folded our comics.

When we were done eating, Peter and I pushed our chairs out and walked away, sometimes still reading, leaving Dad alone to finish his supper, clear the table and wash the dishes. We adjourned to the TV room to watch *Howdy Doody, The Cisco Kid, Superman,* or *The Range Rider* now brought into our home by television.

Watching TV

Despite the screams of the Peanut Gallery, it was quiet for Dad. When TV tables came into play, we no longer sat at his table. We ate in front of the TV!

Dad washed the dishes and never asked us to help. I am not sure why. My guess is that he wanted to give us time to do something new and different, something he never had a chance to do. Or maybe he liked his quiet time after a busy and stressful day at work. He understood and accepted that Mom needed to work for her family and her renewal. She was recovering from a serious thyroid illness and regaining confidence by working.

I believe that it was a transformative time for all of us. Mom needed to heal and our family needed more money.

I am not sure what happened to those books. Somehow, they went missing. Maybe Dad threw them out in a purge. Maybe I did. I know that when I first realized they were gone. I could have cried.

The Devil Dog

I loved Oreos, hermits, napoleons, cornets, zeppole, banana splits, sfogliatelle, chocolate éclairs, lemon squares, fig squares, Drumsticks and a frozen Charleston Chew. But The Devil Dog was my all-time, extra-special favorite after school snack. Mom kept a stash on the shelf of the metal Tip Top Bread box in the pantry. I started thinking of the "Dog" as soon as the last bell rang. It had been a while since lunch, and I needed something to ready me for my after school games.

The Devil Dog was a work of art, composed of two pieces of dark brown, firm cake no more than six inches long and three inches wide, holding between them the best white frosting ever. Each Dog was wrapped in its own waxed paper home.

I hurried down the driveway, opened the outside door, bolted up three flights of stairs, threw open the door, leaped into the kitchen, made a quick right turn to the pantry, stopped, lifted the lid of the bread box, removed my Devil Dog, unwrapped it, scrunched the paper, threw it in the basket under the sink and then lay the Dog down.

Next, I opened the refrigerator, took out a bottle of Mt. Pleasant Dairy milk, tapped the refrigerator door shut, flipped the top off the milk, took a Howdy Doody glass from the shelf, poured the glass full and left the bottle on the counter. With both hands full, I marched to the kitchen table and sat next to the window. The afternoon sun lit Grandpa's garden below.

Between the cakes of the Dog was a layer of soft, mushy whiteness, like a warm version of soft serve ice cream. It squished out when I squashed the cakes. On the rare occasion when I had a Dog rather than a Twinkie for my school lunch snack, if Mom did not place it in the lunch bag on top of my baloney sandwich, it squashed so that the cream escaped the cakes to the confines of the wrapper. The Dog was sensitive. I licked the wrapper clean. The cream was too good to waste.

There was a variety of ways to eat the Dog. Most often I bit the end, washed it down with the milk and licked my fingers. The key was not to squeeze the "Dog" too hard or the cream would escape. I became an expert at the gentle squeeze. That's how I ate the Dog most often, with a soft squeeze to keep the cream oozing slightly around the rim and then the chomp. There was nothing worse than eating a broken Dog. With large bites, I twirled the mixture of cake, cream and milk in my mouth before I gulped it down.

On a rare occasion, I took the Dog apart and attacked each half, licking cream off from end to end and side to side. Following that, I stuffed one whole side of the naked cake into my mouth, again washing it down with cold milk and repeating the process with the other cake. When done, I gulped the remnants of milk. At other times, I dunked the Dog in the milk, but it became too mushy and pieces broke off into the glass.

The Devil Dog, with a variety of options that always yielded its reward, was a treat to remember.

The Party Line

We had no privacy. There were people on our telephone! That's right; four households, ours and three others, using the same line. We had no choice, either because we did not know any better or needed to save money. My guess, the latter. One other thing. All three families in our three-decker used the same phone, a burly, black, rotary table model that sat on the mahogany linen chest in the dining room of my grandparents' tenement.

Party line conversations were sometimes shared unbeknownst to those on a call. It was not uncommon to pick up the phone to hear someone talking. I was compelled to listen, though most, if not all, of the time,

I never heard anything important or cryptic like an air-raid or an enemy sub off the Narragansett shore. I snooped by wriggling my finger under the phone and over the cradle to hold it down while lifting ever so slowly. All I ever heard was chitchat and idle gossip.

"Did someone just click in?" Drat. I pressed back down like a dormouse. Easy to do when you are invisible. When I succeeded and the chatterboxes were unaware, maybe I heard stuff like this:

"I'm not sure why she got so upset. All I said was she had a nice outfit, considering."

"Well, you know, Mom, she just had a baby."

"Sure I do, but what has that got to do with her being upset? This should be a happy time for her."

"She gained a lot of weight. Why did you say 'considering'?"

"Considering? Considering? I wasn't even aware I said it."

"There you go again."

God, this was boring. It was time to let them know someone was waiting. Click, click, clicka, click, whoosh and whoosh, the old silent in and out whistle into the phone trick.

"I guess someone wants to use the line. The nerve."

"Yeah, I guess. The nerve. But, you know, I can never figure her out. Why would a simple compliment get her so upset?"

"Cause … you … said … 'considering'."

Click, click, click, clicka, click … "Dammit, I hate this party line!" They slammed their phones.

I hung up gently and picked up. Good, a dial tone. I called Dan who lived around the corner. "Hi, Mrs. Falls, is Dan there?" Was that a click I heard?

"Yes, justa minute, Eddie."

"Hi, Ed."

"Hi Dan. Are you going to the movies tonight?" Silence.

"Yeah." Silence. We were not phone conversationalists. Another pause.

"Are Patti and Marie goin'? By the way, do you hear something?" Another pause.

"Yeah, I think. Uh, no, I don't hear anything." Now this was meaningful conversation. Pause.

"Do you think you're goin' ta the Creamery after the movie?" Click, click, clicka, click and whoosh.

Now who could that be? "Hey, who's tryin' ta break in here? Nosy?

Are ya nosy or somethin'? Give us a minute here. Dan, someone wants the phone, I guess. The nerve."

"Yeah, the nerve. OK. Meet ya at 5:30." Pause. Click.

Silence. "OK, here's ya dam phone."

One day, I got a call. My grandmother called up the stairs. "Ed-a wood. Ed-a-wood. Somaoneonathefonefayou." When I walked through her kitchen to the dining room, I noticed a thin smile as she stopped sweeping to watch me pass. "Why does she have that look?" I wondered as I turned the corner to the dining room and swung the door closed. I waited a moment.

I picked the phone up, waited a moment and answered, "Uh, ha–llo."

"Hi Eddie. It's Marie." Ah, a girl. The reason for Grandma's smile.

"Hi, Marie."

"Are you going to the Castle tonight?" I could picture Marie, my beautiful friend with such a smooth voice.

"Uh, I'm not sure." Tongue tied again. In the moment, I forgot what Dan and I had planned.

"OK. If you decide to go, can you call me?"

"Sure, what's your number?"

"Do you have something to write on?" Now I was more flustered. No pencil. No paper.

"Yeah, sure. Go ahead."

She gave it to me. "You won't forget it, will you?"

"Nope," as I was scratching the number into the top of Grandma's linen chest with my jackknife. For sure, I'll never forget it.

"See ya." I hung up and took a look. It was there. A telephone number scratched into the mahogany. *I* did it. I was screwed. What would Grandma think about the lasting erosion in her beautiful chest? I had to confess because Dad would figure it was me by calling the number when the screaming started. With heavy, sticky sneakers, I trudged up the stairs.

The next day, Grandma was waiting, leaning on her broom as I passed by her open door. She stared and said nothing. She didn't have to. Italian Grandmas let you know how much trouble you are in with just *that look*.

I scurried down two stairs at a time, doomed forever to phone prohibition.

There was more party line stuff. Cousin Mike said. "If you call your own number and hang up right away, all the phones ring at the same time and everyone will answer." I did it. Ours rang. I picked up to a choral "Hello?" It worked!

Party lines were not supposed to be fun, but they were. It ended when we went to our own 'private' line. Mom and Dad were so proud. Privacy and the phone in our space. It came at the same time as our first television. There was no reason to eavesdrop or tussle for time ever again. We had a TV and a single party line.

I would never have dreamed that today everyone would have their own telephone to carry. What if I were born in the day of the cell phone and text message?

Why, I would have missed all the fun.

The Music Goes Round and Round

Music can relax you, move you to another place. You listen and soar to another world, round and round, and it comes out somewhere, but who knows where. Bill Haley and the Comets did it for me years ago. So did Carl Perkins, Red Prysock and others. So too does opera, jazz, country and zydeco today.

Here is a recent memory from my youth.

Our third-floor tenement was full of sunshine. On Saturday mornings, Mom listened to the radio WHIM and DJ Bob LaChance. Bob's enthusiasm, singing and music added to the glow. She loved him.

Mom did housework and sang along with Bob on those Saturdays. She danced as she was making the bed and sang at the top of her voice. Unlike my Dad who, if he ever sang did it in monotone, Mom was good, though I did not appreciate her early morning march singing "Onward Christian Soldiers" to wake us on school days.

One Saturday, Bob introduced a tune that was entertaining and fun. As I recall, this is what he said. "I'm going to play a real oldie that many of you may remember. Here goes." He played "The Music Goes Round and Round," big band stuff with Tommy Dorsey.

"I love that song," Mom warbled. "Your Dad and I danced to it years ago. In fact, it was so popular that one radio station played it all day."

Bob, a tenor, sang along with the Dorsey band. Mom accompanied him.

I blow through here
The music goes round and around
Whoa-ho-ho-ho-ho

And it comes out here.
I push the first valve down
The music goes down and around
Whoa-ho-ho-ho-ho
And it comes out here
Listen to the jazz come out
I push the other valve down
The music goes round and around …

"Round and round? Mom, what's he singing about?"

Just as the song ended, Bob commented, "This is a song about a tuba. You blow in the mouthpiece, and the music goes around and around and comes out the big bell." Of course. I wondered if the marcher staggering beneath the weight of his tuba was comforted knowing that his puffs went round and round to glory.

Years later, I was working at the City Hall Hardware Store for Christmas and heard a distinctive tenor voice behind me "Do you mind waiting on me? I have a question." I knew immediately who it was.

"Sure, sure," I replied, turning and blurting, "I know who you are!"

He was smaller than I thought. He was wearing a black topcoat and black soft hat; dressed, not at all like what I thought a disc jockey should because, you see, he was Bob LaChance. Then again, I never thought about what disc jockeys wear. The voice was the only thing that mattered.

"You do? How?"

"My mother listened to you every Saturday morning and sang along with you. I recognize your voice. I remember you playing 'The Music Goes Round and Round.'"

"You remember that? Why, thank you." He was pleased. I liked him.

Round and round. Really. Just the other day, I thought of the song. It reminded me of what music can do for you; it makes you go round and round to another world and out of yours. I tapped my fingers

whoa, ho ho ho ho, ho … and it comes out here.

Yes, it comes out here or wherever, who knows.
Maybe still back into the sunny tenement?

I Needed to Drive

The idea excited me, made me one of the guys with a story to tell. I wanted to drive when I was fourteen, and I wanted to drive a car with a stick shift. There was something about the rhythm, timing and power of shifting a car that captivated me. My father traded in his car for a Power Glide Chevrolet, so the only shift car I knew was my uncle's truck.

Uncle Carlo's truck was a blue '49 Dodge two door, panel with two cloth seats in the front and a bay in the rear to carry groceries for his customers. Because of his passion for driving in the snow, he used the truck during storms. When a northeaster was on its way he said, "Let's put the chains on the truck. We'll pull people out." And off we went to help people stuck in the snow. When my feet were cold, my chest was warm and when my feet were warm, I was cold. A whirring fan under the panel blew cold air. The temperature didn't matter.

I watched him maneuver, not the truck but the clutch and the shift. That was the exciting part. An ever present cigar in his mouth, the smell pervasive, he would push the clutch in with his left foot, pull the shift into first, step on the gas with the right foot, wind it out, push the clutch, shift into second, step on the gas, wind it out, push the clutch, shift down to third, foot on the gas and off we went. Sometimes he would skip steps and go from first to third or second to fourth, I think. These were world class moves. Backing the truck up meant putting the shift in another place all together. To drive like that was my desire, but I had two more years before I could get my license.

Uncle Carlo parked his truck in front of our house when he went in for lunch. Sometimes he took a nap. Almost always, he left a huge bunch of keys hanging on a ring in the ignition, doors unlocked. No one ever removed keys or locked doors in those days. Maybe I could drive the truck just a little way. One day I felt bold enough to try.

I looked in. The keys were in the ignition! I looked at the house. I looked up and down the street. It was a quiet, hazy summer afternoon, and the only thing I heard was the drone of insects we called sewing bees.

I opened the door and sat behind the wheel. I took a deep breath. The familiar smell of cigar emanated from the upholstery and mingled with the odors of oil, groceries, wood crates and onions. Above the visor was a package of Dutch Masters. I cradled the keys and wiggled in the seat. I closed the door. I put both hands on the steering wheel. I looked right, left, and then to the rear. With a stretch, I could see the Ram's head hood ornament. I looked in the mirror at a small rear window.

OK, time to give it a try. My plan was to drive the truck up a few feet then back a few feet, then up, then back. I fingered the keys again, stretched my left foot and pushed it down on the clutch as far as I could. It was a long way. I was at the edge of the seat. I peeked above the wheel, took a deep breath and turned the key. The truck started with a crank, crank, va-da-ruum and then a purr, ka-chug, ka-chug.

I pulled the shift hard into first like my uncle did. As I turned to look around, my foot slipped back, off the clutch and giddyap ... off I went, like Hopalong Cassidy trying to tame a stallion. Ka-boom, ka-boom, screech, screech, lurch, back, neck jolted, boxes in the rear jumping forward and back again, chugging by the streetlight and the front of the house, not having a clue about what to do next. I turned the key and the bucking stopped with the truck now in a different place. I could feel my heart thumping. I started to sweat. I was a goner.

The neighborhood's quiet was disturbing. I expected the doors of every house to open. I waited. Nothing. No one. Now what? I had to get back to the original spot.

I pushed the clutch in, toes to the floor, turned the key and started the truck again. With a few chugs, the engine purred. But where was reverse? I had to put the shift in reverse, and I had not seen it done that often. I remember my uncle pushing the shift up, so I did it, looked back at the rear window, now even smaller, and let the clutch out slowly enough to avoid the bucking. It was smooth. But I was not going backward, I was going forward! I had the clutch in second speed! I turned the key and stopped. Now, I was beyond my house and in front of Mr. Rossini's, next door. I was done. How was I to get the truck back to its original position? I sat, ready to cry, and then came my savior.

Wally exited his house and spotted me behind the wheel. "What's going on?" he chuckled. I told him.

"Let's see if we can get this thing back to where it was." Wally got in the truck, pushed the clutch, wiggled the shift into a loose position, neutral, and got out, leaving the door open. He turned to the rear with one hand on the wheel and the other on the door jam. He bent his knees and rounded his shoulders.

"Get in front," he said. "Push! Hard!" The truck started its roll. We pushed it close to its original position.

"There," said Wally. "See ya." He walked back to his house.

"Thanks." My hero.

I sat on the steps of the porch, elbows on my knees and hands on my sweaty chin until Uncle Carlo came out. He went to his truck, started the engine, pulled forward, leaned over and rolled down the passenger window. "Were you in this truck?"

"Uh yeah."

He smiled, let out the clutch and purred down the street.

I Learn to Drive the Power Glide and the Austin Healey at Ten and Two

Ever since Dad sat me on his lap and had me hold the steering wheel as he drove, I wanted to drive. I wanted to drive a stick shift, but Dad had a jet-black, four-door '54 Chevy Power Glide. "I can't believe I drove a shift car all those years." Dad said, "I love it. I'll never get anything else."

Dad traded his cars every two years. His round trip to work of over 60 miles with five passengers took its toll. His car had a spicy smell with a hint of nicotine. The floor mats were clean. He changed the oil every 1000 miles, checked the spark plugs, kept the gas tank filled and added dry gas in the winter. In anticipation of a snowstorm, he put chains on the tires, jacking the rear end himself. He washed and polished it squeaky clean every week. The trunk was spotless. "If you take care of a car, it will take care of you," was his oft-heard phrase.

He screwed a St. Christopher medal above the driver's side, reminding me often that St. Christopher was the patron saint of travel.

He was proud of his low number plate, L49, a Rhode Island status symbol. How did this working man get it since he was neither famous nor a politician? His friend and local council member, Tommy L (L50) arranged it.

Dad loaded the car for summer Sunday trips to the beach, took it to visit his sisters and boyhood chums and went for winter Sunday rides with Mom, ending with a window-shopping 'spin' through downtown Providence.

As methodical as he was in caring for his car, so too was he in his teaching. "Open the door, settle in the seat, close the door, pull up the seat so you can reach, put the key in, put your hands on the wheel at the ten and two, keep it in park, start it with your foot on the brake, lower the emergency, look left, look right, look in the mirror, watch the other guy, etc.

1954 Chevy

He showed me how to change a flat, but the first time I did it alone, I parked too close to the curb and took the lugs off before I realized I could not get the tire off. (That's for another story.)

"Ok, get in," he said. I slid onto the cloth seats and looked out the two-paneled windshield. I felt my father's contour and smelled his cigar. I looked in the mirror.

"Don't flood it, easy on the gas. If you flood it, push the gas to the floor and hold it there as you turn the ignition. Keep an eye on the instrument panel, look around and fix the seat." On he went.

After I drove a number of times to and around the high school parking lot, he was confident enough to let me to go for my license. "See if you can set it up with Jerry. He's a friend of mine." To the registry I went.

"I'm here for my driving test," I said to the man at the counter. "Is Jerry here?"

"Sure son, that's me. I'm Jerry. How can I help?"

"I'm here for my driving test.

"OK. Give me a minute. Where's the car?"

"Uh, I parked it alongside the building." Remembering Dad's warning not to get boxed in, I glided it into a space with plenty to spare.

I waited an eternity until Jerry said, "OK. Let's go." I walked alongside him. Because I looked so young, I wondered what he thought. "Uh, oh," I muttered as I spotted the car. Boxed in like a sardine in a can, it looked like the only way I could get the car out was to have it air lifted.

"Uh here we are. The car's right there." I pointed.

"You're driving that Chevy Power Glide?"

"Yes, Sir." Uh oh. What did he mean?

"Kind of a tough space. How'ja get in there?"

"Uhhh …"

"Never mind. Good job. I love this car," he beamed. "I'm still driving a shift, but one day, I'll have an automatic. Is it a six or an eight?"

"A six or an eight?" What the heck was he talking about? "Uh yeah, yep. It's great. My Dad loves it."

"OK, never mind, get in." The doors closed with the clung of something made well. He sat in the passenger seat. Until then, I never realized how close it was. I could hear his breathing and smell his aftershave and cigarettes. "Let's go."

I went through Dad's ritual … sit comfortable in the seat, key in ignition, foot on the brake, emergency brake down, hands at ten and two, take the right hand off to start the car. At that point I froze. How will I get this car out of this space with the bumpers of the adjacent cars near touching? I looked ahead; tight. I looked to the left; small street. I looked to the right; sidewalk. I looked to the rear; tight. I double jiggled the emergency brake. I put my hands at ten and two again. I checked the rear mirror. I fussed in the seat. HE was silent, watching, his breathing more audible. I prayed he didn't notice my tremble or hear my pounding heart. I felt his eyes.

I looked to the spot between our seats where years ago I stood when

Dad drove. When braking, he interrupted my forward thrust by bracing me with his strong right arm, all the while commanding the wheel with his left hand.

"Ok, start her up." I did, keeping my left at ten and quickly moving my right off the two spot to the key in the ignition, turned it and quickly returned my right to the two. Jerry had to love that move.

"Let's go." I choked the wheel. He glanced at my application just as I was about to put the car in reverse. He turned and asked, "Wait, is your Dad Pete?"

"Yes."

"Great guy."

"Yes, he is."

"OK, turn the car off. You pass." Never moving the car, I had my license. Ahh, the friend at the state agency. I was not about to complain. "Come on back to the registry. I'll get your stuff ready." I walked with a bounce, feeling taller and grown-up.

He handed me the papers. I looked at my license. It did not say Limited to Automatic. Yes! I could still drive a shift. When I returned to the car, I was still boxed in but maneuvered out with the skill of a racecar driver. A car sped by. I avoided it, not touching the brake as I tapped the wheel and thumped the dash with confidence. I leaned forward, now with my hands at eight and four. I turned on the radio with the four hand to 1290 WICE my favorite. Bill Haley and the Comets ... *"One, two, three o'clock, four o'clock rock."* I loved it, so I turned the volume up and the windows down for the world to hear. I cruised home in minutes. *"Five o'clock, six o'clock, seven o'clock rock ... we're gonna rock around the clock all night."*

"How did you do?"

"I passed. It was easy. Oh, and Jerry said to say hello."

Dad smiled. "Good job."

My first drive alone gave me the feeling of freedom. I drove like Dad with my left arm hanging out the window and my right hand at twelve. He would never allow it, but since he did it, so did I. I returned along Wealth Avenue, swerving as the road unfurled below me. Houses which stood so still when I walked to school, now fled by, soon to disappear. Dad was watching from our porch. He called down to me as I pulled up. "Why were you swerving?" I looked up.

"To avoid the potholes." I wanted to show him that I knew how to drive with skill.

"Don't do that again."

"OK."

"And keep your arm in."

When I graduated from high school, Dad bought me an Austin Healey. I loved the car. It was a maroon, 4-door British toy with yellow signal arms that stuck out from between the front and rear doors. The car had a floor shift with a sensitive clutch. This clutch was a real test as I stalled often, scared to death every time I stopped and had to go again. "Light off the clutch, don't ride it, light on the gas, timing, timing," Dad said. The car burned oil like gasoline, so that every time I stepped on the gas, a cloud of profuse, pungent smoke filled the air. I learned how to check the oil and always stashed a case in the trunk.

The real test of driving was on College Hill near Brown University. The traffic light was at the peak. I stopped. A car came behind and stopped, sealing me in. Too close, dammit, too close. "Back up, I have a tender clutch," I yelled, but he never heard me.

The light changed. I took a deep breath. Light off the clutch, heavier than usual on the throttle ... vroom, vroom, sputter, buck ... toxic oil everywhere. I was rolling back, back, too very near. Brake. Stall. Clutch in, foot on the brake. Start the car. Light off the clutch, move that foot, light on the gas ... grind ... putter ... whine ... vroom, vroom. Heavier on the gas. As I revved it, the tires screeched and the car cranked out a stream of heavy oil in a blast of noxious fumes pouring under his car, over the hood to his windshield. Bucking and lurching ... hut, hut, hut ... I shot forward and up the hill. I looked back at the guy lost in the cloud, sponge dice hanging from his mirror, a fist waving out the window. I whipped up to the next light.

I had passed the sensitive clutch test.

I putted along with my hands at ten and two, a stream of white trailing. The Austin and I were one.

Hands Like Papa's

"Edward, you have hands like Papa's," Aunt Della blurted. "I can't believe it." Nor could I, though I'm sure she meant it as a compliment. She loved her father, respecting how hard he worked, but I would never have the hands of a man who did manual labor like him.

Papa was my grandfather. His hands were heavy, knuckley, gnarly and calloused. At ten, mine were soft, clean and except for a small knob on the side of my inner second finger where I choked the pen to write, had no calluses.

Perhaps Papa's hands were trying to tell me something of what I might or should be one day. His were the hands of hard work; crooked, grubby, dirt under the nails, bruised with cuts, and with brown spots on the back that resembled the map of Europe. I watched him make cement one day. He was patching a square under our grape arbor.

As I watched him stirring the cement ... sand, water, stones ... mixing, testing, eventually pouring ... I was transfixed because I knew this slurry would toughen to indestructibility. And I knew that at some moment, just before it hardened, he might let me scratch my name in his masterpiece.

I looked in his toolbox. It was not a box but a leather bag, cracked and crusted with dust, hardened plaster and cement. He was a cement worker in the days of the depression, given a chance to work by President Roosevelt's WPA. In the toolbox were a hammer, a spade and all those things necessary to smooth, set and define cement.

"Grandpa, how do you know how to do all this stuff ... make cement, build a shed, plant a garden, bury a tree?" I thought of the fig tree he covered every autumn and released every spring.

He paused, turned his head and looked up from his kneeling position. "I learna what I hafata. I makea what I hafata makea to helpa the family. You no wanna do this, Ed-a-wood. You wanna go to the school. Looka." He put his tools down, slapped his hands together, spewing dust, and rotated those hands, palms to the sky. Those palms were as knotty, thick, scarred and as tough as the cement he was creating. Some wisps had seeped into the cracks. His fingers were bent.

"Thisa from harda work Ed-a-wood. I like-a to do. Mah, you. You must-a stay inna the school. Giva me your hand." His hand was rough, moist and warm. He took my hand, spread my fingers and pushed it into the wet, cold, setting cement. He held it there for a moment and then released it. I looked. My hand was imprinted into the cement that when dry, would be there forever on that slab in the rear yard under the grapevine. I looked at my palm. It looked a little like grandfather's.

When the slab was done, it was the only section under the arbor with no grape stains and with a handprint, mine. Under it he scratched, "Edward, 1949."

"Thanks, Grandpa." He smiled.

The other day, I looked at my hands, palms up. They were still soft, smooth and were a reflection of a lifetime in one school or another. I turned them over and looked at the backs. Prominent veins, spots and wrinkles now crept into what once was smooth and unblemished. They bruise easily and the bruises turn brown and the brown lingers. My knuckles seem bigger.

Now, at least on the dorsal sides, I have hands like Papa's. Aunt Della, I have hands like Papa has, not gnarled or crooked, just exposed and aged.

I understand what you meant when you said I had hands like Papa's. I would love to return to the yard to see if my handprint is still there.

May 1946

Polenta

Grandma was at the stove stirring something in a large pot. From that pot popped bubbles of vapor giving the kitchen air a nutty aroma of our beloved gravy. In another pot, she was making polenta. I was not excited because she wanted me to eat it.

When she was done, she plopped a lump of the yellow gruel onto a board that almost spanned the kitchen table. Grandma then smushed the middle and ladled a large dollop of gravy onto the mound. Grandpa pulled his chair closer. Grandma turned to me, standing at her open door with one foot outside.

Waving her gravy laden spoon toward the board and motioning with the other hand, she spoke, "Ed-a-wood. Come in. Come in. Mangia, mangia. Hav-a some *pullend"* (dialect). "Tsa gooder for you."

I tried it once, but it was too dry and tasteless. Adding more gravy didn't help. As the polenta dried, its edges hardened, and I broke a small piece to dip in the gravy. That was a little better, but to sit at the table was not for me. I had more important things to do.

Mom said that polenta was the porridge that Goldilocks and the three bears enjoyed. "You should taste it, Edward. It really is good."

Sure, the bears ate it. So did the Italians. There was nothing else in those dark days in Italy after WWI. It was peasant's food of little or no nutritional value. The corn meal lacked niacin and as a result, outbreaks of pellagra ... confusion, intestinal symptoms, skin rash, sometimes death ... occurred throughout much of Europe. It was one of the many reasons the immigrants left.

'It's gruel, Mom."

"It's not gruel. Its polenta, porridge."

The gruel of a previous century had a bad rap. It was boiled in milk or water. Inmates of prisons and other institutions were forced to eat it. Gruel was made famous by Dickens's Oliver Twist, the little orphan boy in the workhouse who was so hungry, he asked for seconds.

History was of no matter when it came to Grandpa's love of polenta. He pulled up to the table, spooned large dollops into his plate, used the same spoon to ladle more gravy from the pan, took a hunk of Italian bread, usually the heel (candozza, dialect) and slurped up his meal while he read the local Italian newspaper, The Echo, aloud. I wondered if it brought back memories of his youth.

Polenta has come a long way since those peasant days of the immigrants, since grandma cooked it, since the three bears and Oliver Twist ate it and since the day I avoided it.

It is now a tasty offering in many restaurants; not runny, lumpy or tasteless. Ricotta in the mix helps its texture and moisture. It is prepared in any number of ways – fried, squares served at cocktail parties, with mushrooms, rabe, arugula, etc.

I like it. I pay for it.

I wonder what grandpa would say if he saw the price of a dish of his *pullend* today.

Ramblings from One Who Never Smoked. I Tried

I grew up with the pervasive smell of cigarettes. It seemed everyone smoked. Even today, the smell triggers memories of boxing matches, neighborhood corners, cars, uncles and Dad.

There was smoke everywhere; in homes, stores, theaters, the church basement and the Arena, where you could cut the smoke with a knife at hockey games or boxing matches. Ceilings held smoke in clouds. Cigarettes glowed like fireflies in the dark on a porch across the street, puffs of white circling their way to the sky. Smokers held cigarettes between fingers that surrounded a coffee mug. Lipstick encircled a butt in an ashtray.

The odor was inescapable and offensive. Cars smelled of smoke. Teachers smelled of smoke. The reek could blunt the scent of mothballs. At the local bar, where men held a beer and a cigarette in the same hand, the air was riddled with the unpleasant smell. One last puff and a stomp with the heel of a shoe; another squashed butt on a floor. Or those huddled in the cold, one hand in a pocket, trying to stay warm with a cigarette in the other. Really?

Chain smokers had nicotine stains high up between the first and second knuckles, yellow moustaches and yellow teeth. Fingers held cigarettes with care and confidence, flicking thumbs and digits, waving hands sideways nonchalantly while leaning back and blowing smoke with a volcano-like whoosh. A cigarette behind an ear. One held joyously between the teeth. One flipped from corner to corner.

Old Gold, Lucky Strike, Pall Mall, Chesterfield, Camels, Kool's, Philip Morris, Benson and Hedges, Herbert Tareytons. Kids could buy cigarettes.

My uncle asked me to buy two packs of Tareytons for him. He saved the coupons.

Soft or hard pack? Hard packs protected the cigarettes from being crushed. Marlboros came in a hard pack. College classmates collected them for prizes. A friend opened his hefty desk drawer to display his stash of empty boxes. "Prizes, you know. Empty boxes for prizes." Lucky him. Maybe.

There were slogans:

"I'd walk a mile for a mild, mild Camel. They're so mild they suit you to a tee."

"Tareyton smokers would rather fight than switch." Really? They should have switched.

How about LSMFT? *"Lucky Strike Means Fine Tobacco."*

"Call for Philip Morr … ees," the little guy screeched on the commercial of the TV show *Hit Parade.* He wore a box of Philip Morris as he roamed the crowd.

Announcer Dennis James sold Old Golds with the catch phrase, "Old Gold. OK? O … K."

There were rituals.

How to open a pack. Invert and tamp the pack or rap it against your palm. Carefully remove the cellophane using the handy tab and rip the tinfoil top enough to reveal the cigarettes. Remove the first cigarette and reverse it so that the end to be lit was sticking up.

How to hold a cigarette. Between the index and middle finger, between the first and second knuckle, palm facing downward (palmed), a cigarette pinched between thumb and forefinger, palm facing in and cigarette secreted in a hand pointing towards the inner wrist. Useful (maybe) when you don't want it to be obvious that you're smoking.

How to smoke a cigarette.

Don't smoke it to the end! Don't Bogart it! Have a drag. Take a short drag. Drag on this. Don't wet it! It's "fish-lipped" and disgusting.

Jimmy could blow smoke rings. He pursed his lips and out came a row of perfect circles, like the guy on the billboard in Times Square.

Mikey could take a drag through his nostril. Ugh.

Some let the smoke dribble, exhaling slowly to let the trickle track along the upper lip and back in through the nose.

Three on a match, good luck. Four better.

They lit punk, salutes, sparklers and other cigarettes from the lit one. Some used them to pay off card debts, throwing cigarettes at the pile of money.

Another sport. "OK, c'mere, Ed. Watch the smoke come out of my ears," said uncle. I moved closer. He inhaled and told me to concentrate on his ears? As I did, he grabbed my calf. "Horse bit ya, huh? Ha, ha, ha, ha, horse bit ya," laughing in staccato, blowing puffs out of his nose.

Dad said smoking was an awful, filthy and expensive habit impossible to shake. He smoked two packs of Chesterfields a day. His words stuck, but at every turn, I was tempted. One day, at the urging of friends and wanting to be cool, I tried.

I was in junior high school when I bought my first pack of Chesterfields. I rolled the pack up in the sleeve of my tee shirt and swaggered across the George J. West baseball field. I approached a group sitting on one of the benches. I offered. I wanted to be one of the boys, accepted.

"Eddie, you don't smoke, do you?"

"No, but I wanna start," I replied, looking at the ground, twirling the toe of my shoe in a circle in the dirt.

"OK. Good. We'll tell ya how. Ya gotta inhale ta get over it. Jes do it. Y'll probly get sick the first time, but y'll get over it fast." Did I detect a smirk?

I took the cellophane off, opened the corner of the pack and tapped it on the back of my hand. A few staggered out. They each took one. I put one in my mouth and let it hang a bit, reached into my pocket, took out a match-book, opened the cover, tore off a match, looked around, struck it by pulling it between the cover and the surface and lit my cigarette. I took a puff, held it in my mouth and then blew a soft wisp to the sky. Not so bad.

"Ya gotta inhale. Ya gotta suck it in all the way ta the bottom of yer lungs. Take a big drag and suck it in."

I took a drag, rolled the smoke around my mouth and with pursed lips took the ultimate smokers inhalation … a sucking hiss, like a vacuum. The smoke climbed my palate, scratched my throat and slid down my windpipe. Into my lungs it passed with the force of a blowtorch.

A small cough progressed quickly to consecutive whoops. I stumbled, bent over, dropped to my knees, coughed more ferociously and yorked my lunch. Snort, snort, bubbles of green mucus came out of my nose. My eyes watered so that I could not see, tears streaming down my cheeks. I broke into a cold sweat. My chest tightened. Is this what smoking is all about? Oh, my God, the pain. I thought the vicious coughing, retching and flushing would never end. I became a spectator sport for the benchwarmers. Giggles rose to laughter. "Now ya got it."

I finally controlled it. I stood up slowly, took the pack, ripped open the top, turned it upside down, scattered the cigarettes in front of the snickering herd and stomped on them with the heaviness of a horse's hoof. I churned them into the ground with the sole of my right shoe. Paper scattered along with the flecks of tobacco. I tossed the matches.

"Hey, what are ya doin'? Good cigarettes. What are ya doin'?" I turned and walked away from cigarettes, forever. So what?

So what! I risked something catastrophic and survived. That's what!

I came home reeking of smoke and vomit. "What happened?" asked Dad. He smiled. He knew.

Now, a long time after, I reflect on those days, days when I wanted to be accepted. As a physician, I witnessed the ravages of cigarettes, thinking of my father, father-in-law, uncles, and friends; those who succumbed with heart attacks, aneurysms, strokes, bladder, neck and lung cancers …
diseases that killed them, often too slowly and with too much agony. I took care of them, and it was difficult.

Although I did not know it in my youth and for some years thereafter, this is what I think now. Yes, cigarettes were bad, and I was lucky to never start. With smoking, there is failure that belies research and knowledge. There is a sorrow that topples joy. We have failed.

I also reflect upon my need to be accepted, to join the group, to start my journey to becoming grown-up. So I tried something that I was warned by Dad not to do. "Never start to smoke." He was so right.

Being one of the guys nearly did me in. It took years for the lesson to sink.

CHAPTER THREE

THE NEIGHBORHOOD

Hot Summer Nights

Summer days could be hot enough to fry an egg on the sidewalk. We cooled under sprinklers or swam at the Olneyville Boys Club. We made tar balls from hot tar we scraped off the steaming streets. Sewing bees sewed and lightning bugs flickered on their evening soirees. Nights in the third-floor bedroom of our three-decker could be unbearable.

With no air conditioners, our bedroom was a clammy oven. Sleeping was difficult. Adjacent homes were close and only a rare breeze trickled through. The air was sluggishly stirred by struggling fans. Nevertheless, those nights lent themselves to soothing memories.

The heat drove the adults to their porches. Hearing soft chatter from the first-floor porch below, Peter and I decided to follow the murmurs and soft laughter.

Attracted by the sound as bees to honey, we rolled out of bed and snuck down the stairs to sit shirtless on the porch floor off to the side. Mom, Aunt Della and Grandma glanced at us and continued talking. As I remember, Mom was in her pajamas, Aunt Della in a nightgown and Grandma in a housedress and backless black slippers.

The moonlight and layers of stars sprinkled the clear night. More light came from a nearby streetlight, bugs flickering to tap the light's metal hat. Shadows from the trees and houses painted the street. Rumbling came from neighbors sitting nearby. They too were chatting away the heat.

The sounds were comforting as people made the best of the heat. They were used to much tougher situations.

We sat still, moving only to smush a mosquito. "Time for bed kids." Up we went.

We dozed to the ongoing music of the voices below.

I Yield to Temptation Over a Walnut. OK, I Stole Something

A walk of two blocks past the firefighter's gray bungalow, past the squat house where the motor cycle brothers rumbled out their driveway and past the seminarian's home was the store.

It was a small neighborhood market like those on almost every corner. Painted red, the building supported a tenement above where the owner lived. Ceiling fans reverberated. Its narrow aisles were packed with dry goods. A refrigerator full of meats and cheese stood to one side. There was a tall cooler for soda, bins full of vegetables, and in the front window were boxes of grapes, oranges apples and nuts. A picker pole hung by a hook.

I loved the smells of onions, cheese, bread, flour, dried beans, cardboard, eggs and sausage. The white, bubbled ceiling supported fluorescent lights that made people look ghostly. Little old ladies wearing shiny black dresses shopped. Men smoking stogies stood around to chat. I heard some Italian. Nehi soda was all I ever bought there. My only other connection with the store was to wax its windows on Halloween.

Mr. F. walked with a slight bend at the shoulders and waist. His milk-white apron was tucked below his armpits and tied in front with a bow. He wore a white, open-collared shirt. My memory of his small face is fuzzy because I never really looked at him, but I think he had a wisp of hair, wore wire-rimmed glasses and sported a small moustache. His eyes were dark and gentle.

This day, after a swig of the Nehi Orange, I looked around and realized I was alone. I looked at the brown, knobby walnuts piled in a box in the window and looking as delicious as a walnut could, I guess. I looked around. It was quiet. I pushed my open hand into the nuts, wiggled it and with two fingers, picked one and dragged slowly.

I heard a shuffle and there he stood, materializing from nowhere, at the counter, near the meat case. Calm, kind and unflappable as in "I have seen this before," he tilted his head, angled his jaw, raised his eyebrow, stared me down and in a soft, priest-like voice, asked, "Canna I help-a you?" He knew. I knew he knew. He knew I knew he knew.

Startled, I pulled my hand back and put it in my pocket, nutless. "No. Uh. I was just checking the nuts." Some comeback. He smiled and wiped his hands on his apron.

"Well, do not touch-a, please." He was such a gentleman. I had the immediate sensations of guilt and shame as in, "What if my father knew?" as in "Stealing is a sin" as in, "I'd better get to confession." I clenched my fist in my pocket, inched back, turned slowly, lowered my head, rounded my shoulders and slinked out of the store strangling my Nehi. I looked up and down the street.

With sins hovering over my head and religious instructions ringing loud and strong, I knew it was time to examine my conscience. This incident came under the "coveting my neighbor's goods" category.

Saturday came with its confession ritual. It was time for restitution; this time not having to make-up sins. I had a real one. I sat alongside a woman with a handkerchief on her head.

When my turn arrived, I entered the musty box, knelt on the hardwood and, head down with hands clasped, rested my wrists on the shelf. The priest rolled back the window, thump. I peaked at his outline silhouetted against the screen, his hand covering his face. I smelled chronic sweat. I don't think it was mine. Good thing he could not see me.

"Yes, son." Darn, he could see me!

"Bless me Father for I have sinned. I disobeyed my mother twice and, and ..."

"Yes." Did I need to tell him about ONE walnut? I was between here and hell. I had no choice.

"I was going to steal a walnut from the grocer, but you know what, Father, I did not."

"And why did you not?" Right. OK. Foiled.

"Uhhh, because he caught me?"

"Well, son, you know that intent to sin is as bad as the sin."

Oh, yeah, sure, I knew that quite well or I would not have mentioned the one, and only, walnut.

"Yes, I do, Father," I whispered.

"OK. Ten Our Fathers, ten Hail Mary's and an Act of Contrition."

"Yikes, steep penance for one unsecured, uneaten walnut," I thought.

"Thank you, Father."

I went to the rail, knelt and proceeded with my Penance. From that moment, whenever I passed the store, I crossed the street. Most would not obsess over this attempted theft of one walnut, but for a long time, it gave me pause.

Somehow, when you've done something wrong, it hangs over you like a fog, whether it's wrong in the eyes of the Lord, the priest, your father or just you.

Swimming in the Box. How to Get Cool and Get Toxins

Niagara Falls it was not. Rather, it was a small dam with a quiet waterfall. The river's water cascaded up to it and slid over, lacking spume and rumble as it tumbled. The sounds were softer, much less than the drumbeat of a big dam. The cement wall built to harness power for the mills upstream was comfortable in the river and seemed to belong there. The swirling water on the upstream side took the shape of an uneven square, so we called it The Box.

The river told another story.

Starting some distance from The Box, it wound and bubbled past its mills. We thought it originated in Olneyville, the small neighborhood of shops and Flynn Towel, the Atlantic Mill, Benny's Home and Auto, the hot wiener place, Jakie Conn's Olympia Movie Theater, the Polish Home, McCarthy's Drug, the Nickerson House and the Boys Club.

Our teacher told us that the river was the Woonasquatucket, originating in North Smithfield not Olneyville, and wound along to join the Moshassuck to form the Providence River before it entered the Atlantic Ocean. We laughed at the sound of the names as she curled them around her tongue and lips ... Wooooon–ask–cua–tuck–it, and Moe–shass–suck. "They are Indian names you know."

The Woon-ask-qua-tuck-it did not have the clean, refreshing sparkle of the summer shore or the swimming hole at Twin Rivers. Rather, intermingled in its clear streams were globs of greenish, oily stuff floating side by side with bubbles, like the soap Mom used when she washed the clothes. Along its bank were bent trees, clumps of grass interspersed with dead animals ... a toad, a snake ... sharing space with rusted parts, a car tire, cans, big rocks, pebbles, sticks and, of course, the foam. We noticed little more than The Box, a place to cool. The consequences of swimming in the mills' effluents were not an issue. How would we know?

We were a bunch of ball-playing, neighborhood kids who were hot, sweaty and dusty and wanted to cool. So we were drawn to The Box after playing in the baking sun at the nearby Valley Street grounds. We ran to the water.

We stripped to our shorts, walked carefully on the mildew and patches of moss on the narrow wall, stood with arms crossed for a moment, then raised them above our heads and dove into the swirling eddies. The shock of cold water had a refreshing tingle. Except for the rustle of the dives and the snorts when we surfaced, it was quiet. If we stopped to listen, we heard the trickle of the river and the rattling rumble of the mills' machines.

In the murky, cold water, we were liberated from the dust and percolating heat. Though the water had a musty smell of a mechanics garage, soap and a dirt cellar ... smells that burned in my nostrils for the day ... it did not matter. The cool water was worth it. Years later, Uncle Al, who grew up in Olneyville and swam there when he was a kid, told me his story.

"There were green things and rats floating by. Polio? Never happened. We never thought about it and never got it. We were tough guys, immune from that stuff. The river made us strong. We just nevah opened our mouths."

I shudder to think of what we were exposed to in that river.

Not long ago, Steve, a long-time dear friend who swam with me in those days, joined me in a nostalgic return to see The Box. We were stunned. An outdoor museum, it was now pristine, a fish ladder, the water clean, clear and sparkling, the ripples like water from a tap.

"It's so clean. I can't believe it. It even sounds clean," said Steve.

This day our box was more inviting; not only the story of the river's history and its return to original which we read on the large shore-side board, but also because we reminisced while enjoying the quiet and our memories. We sat on a bench and played jackknife baseball, looking at each other often, saying little while listening to the peaceful sounds of the river and the swirls in The Box.

The Ice Man

"**W**e need ice, Mr. Ice Man."
Some of our neighbors still had the "ICE" sign in the window but not us. Our icebox, replaced by a Kelvinator, was now in the cellar; a storage place for Mason jars. But the ice man still patrolled the neighborhood for those who had not yet converted.

Mr. Wallace, Wally's grandfather, was the man. He and his wife lived nearby in a small bungalow. Of average height, Mr. Wallace had round shoulders and wore professorial wire-rimmed glasses. Gray hairs sprouted from his ears and nose. His forehead was creased and his short teeth bore a hint of yellow. On workdays, he wore dark green pants with a crease, a matching shirt and high-topped boots buffed to an oily sheen. The brim of his green hat sported the stain of hard work.

When not working, he wore a sweater and the same dark green pants. On his day off, he sat with us kids and some attentive adults on the stoop of a three-decker and told stories of retired baseball players, he being one himself.

With bright glint lighting his eyes, he smiled and drawled, "Wellll … a … I … ahh ra-mem-ba Rabbit Ma-ran-ville. Little guy, ya know." As he spoke, he was energized. His cheeks glowed, his eyes widened and his voice muffled a chuckle … "heh, heh … as he gazed upward. His breath came in short whistles.

"What a play-ya. Once I saw him hit twenty fow-ul balls, ya know, pur-posely fow-a-ling pitch afta pitch 'til he'd git the one he wanted. He jes wore the pitcha down." He tapped his pipe on the step, paused a long moment and continued. "I ra-mem-ba Nap Lajoie, L-A-J-O-I-E is how they spell it, but they say La-Joy-yah, ya know, the kid from Woonsocket, in the Hall a Fame, ya know. Yep … Rabbit, Nap … so many great pla-yas in them days. Let me see that bat."

I handed him my 32 oz. Williams bat. He looked at it, turned it around, read the label "Louisville Slugga, huh?" and cradled it softly as if he were holding a pigeon. He then tightened his hands around it, not quite white-knuckled but close, and waved it in short, horizontal spurts, maybe like the guy Maranville.

We gathered and listened because he deserved respect, but my baseball thoughts were on the Red Sox of the day; Vern Stephens, Dom DiMaggio,

Bobby Doerr, Pesky, Goodman and Ted, of course. Never heard of those other guys.

Mr. Wallace was serious when he worked. His dark green, flatbed truck, smelling of oil and coal and with canvas sides cascading from metal hoops, rumbled up to the six-tenement house and stopped with a hiss. He got out, slammed the door, spun on the thick sole of his boot, walked to the rear, turned his head, and looked up. In one window was a sign. "OK, they need twenty pounds," he mumbled, pipe dangling. He flipped up the canvas, looked into the deep, dark end of the truck, placed his pipe upright along the dry side of the bed, rubbed his palms on his trousers and pulled on his gloves.

Toward the front of the truck were huge blocks of ice covered with a heavy leather tarpaulin. He slid the tarp, spotted the huge cake that he wanted and with a long handled, hooked stick, nailed a glistening piece and slid it toward him. Looking over the top of his glasses, he surveyed the piece with the skill of a surgeon and, with a tilt of his head and a calculating glance, cut a piece from the block using a sharp pick that sent a smooth, piercing shock-wave of white peeling apart the layers. The pick read his mind and followed the line; either a phenomenon of nature or more likely, of Mr. Wallace, the skilled diamond-cutter. He surveyed the result. "Twenty. Jes right."

He replaced the pick in the hip holster on his belt with the efficiency of a gunslinger. I loved to watch him drive that pick through the cake, carving just the right size with small slivers left over for us. With wide eyes, I asked, "Can I try that, Mr. Wallace?" The pick looked like it might be fun and easy.

"No, sorry son. Jes a bit too dangj-a-rus." He flipped me a piece of ice. It was refreshing. Mr. Wallace draped a rubber cover over his right shoulder, grabbed the tongs that hung from the side of the truck, pierced the sides of the block and with a jolt of efficiency, picked up the ice, paused, grunted and swung it around to his right shoulder. Bent toward the ground, with ice water dripping down the rubber cover and hitting the back of his pants and the heel of his leather boot, he climbed the stairs and knocked on the door.

"Who is it?"

"Ice man."

From behind the door, there was a clank of bottles and a barking dog. "Good. Come in." Mr. Wallace melted into the house.

The building was a behemoth of six tenements each with its own porch. Shaded by huge maples, it was an uninviting, gray ship with a tiny front yard of dirt enclosed by a rusted fence and creaky gate. Save for a place for the garbage buckets, there was no rear yard. I delivered papers there. It was easy because I ran up the grainy, dimly lit, bare, worn stairs on one side of tenements, dropping the papers at each stop, went out the porch door, strad-dled the rail, sometimes called to the kids below, "Hey, up here," opened the other porch door and bounded down the stairs, again dropping the papers at the other three. Done. One minute.

Mr. Wallace must have had to maneuver his way through that kitchen with the skill of a racecar driver, collect his money and get on down the stairs. He had to have seen the puddles of melted ice on the kitchen floor; puddles which meant more business.

Smiling, he returned to his truck, replaced the tongs, picked up his pipe, put it in the side of his mouth, closed the canvas, took off his gloves, put them in his back pocket, wiped his hands on his pants, stepped on the run-ning board, got in to the cab, fondled the wheel, turned the key, looked out the window and said, "See ya, kids." Off went the truck, engine rumbling, splashes of water tumbling in its wake.

I sometimes think about Mr. Wallace. Our 'cool' neighborhood ice man was soon to be out of a job when everyone went to the Kelvinator. I doubt that he was disappointed. He had more time for his Red Sox.

And his stories.

The Kellogg's Man with a Stash

As I passed a Kellogg's display on a recent trip to the market, it remind-ed me of the man who lived across the street from me so many years ago; the man whose garage was full of Kellogg's stuff.

Kellogg's cereals started my mornings. I ate corn flakes, but I liked Pep better because of the small buttons of Popeye and the Phantom in the box. Mom practically never bought Pep. "Mom, Pep can give you energy."

"Oh, get off." 'Get off', spoken with a flick of the hand, was Mom's favor-ite reply when she did not agree. "There's more energy in spinach because of the iron. You should eat your spinach. Never mind corn flakes."

Having lost the Pep battle, I was working on a spinach win. "I hate spinach. It has no taste. Plus it is ugly green."

"Popeye eats it. Look how strong he is. His muscles pop when he downs a can, and he beats Bluto to get Olive."

I sensed another loss. I changed my tactic.

"What about Wheaties? Can we get Wheaties? They make you strong."

"No way (another well-used comeback). Spinach is better." Her glance ended that discussion.

"How about Frosted Flakes?"

"No way. Too much sugar. They cost more. You can add sugar to the corn flakes if you think you need to, which you don't by the way." She moved on to shredded wheat, the dry wrapped mounds of straw. She had a thing for shredded wheat, again thinking it was an energy builder like Wonder Bread.

"Mom, it's thick and dry, like cardboard. Worse." I was losing the morning scuffles.

"Try some, Edward. Try some. They're whole wheat with vitamins. Farmers eat shredded wheat. They work non-stop all day with that energy. It's good for them and you." To counteract the dryness, I added blueberries and sugar, waiting while the wheat absorbed the milk and sugar, making it soft and sweet enough for me to cut with the tablespoon. The Kellogg's people got the shredded wheat to stay rolled in a tight swirl that repelled milk. It took much too long to soften. I had stuff to do.

As a distraction, there were Rice Krispies, noted for their snap, crackle and pop. Mom bought them, sometimes. The noises came from the rice that absorbed the milk and put pressure on the air in the pockets causing the "walls" to explode. Pictured on the box in front of me (I liked to look at the pictures while I ate) were the elfin mascots, Snap, Crackle and Pop who accompanied me. As I slurped, they snapped, crackled and popped.

Wally's Dad was a sales representative for the Kellogg's Company, and his garage was full of Kellogg' stuff.

I stood alongside the garage as Mr. P, dressed in a light blue striped suit and wearing brown shoes, a straw hat, white shirt and blue tie, came out of his house, walked to the detached garage, slid the key into the hanging padlock and nudged doors that creaked open like stage curtains. The garage did not disappoint. The treasures hung from the loft and lined the sides and rear of the garage; a world of animated splendor, stuff, jammed so tightly that he barely had room for his two-door Chevrolet wagon,

The cast of characters sang to me. There were posters, boxes of Pep pins, standing ads, little toys and buttons, an old horse and buggy picture, an iron toy horse with its buggy. There was a huge Tony the Tiger poster standing in one corner and a large empty box of Corn Flakes in another. I would have loved any one of them, even just one small pin. He cleared his throat. "Morning." I swayed.

"Good morning, Mr. P." I kept my eyes on him, hoping.

He side-saddled into the garage, barely able to open the door of his beach wagon. He squeezed in, started it, shifted to reverse, looked over his shoulder, backed the car out to straddle the sidewalk and the street, put it in neutral, pulled up the brake, got out leaving the door open, returned to the garage and padlocked my friends back into their prison. He moved slowly and seriously. How could he not care about those treasures? Did he not realize that heroes surrounded him? Did he not notice me standing there? I cared. Could he not have at least flipped me a pin?

I stood smiling with my hands folded behind my back as he returned to the car, slammed the door, backed it on to Maplehurst Avenue and straightened it. He glanced. He had to see me. Did he not notice my begging smile? Maybe today he will give me a present. The day never came. He zoomed down the narrow street, a big box of flakes peering out of his rear window.

Today, I think of that garage wishing that I had some of those treasures. I would give them to my grandchildren and tell them the stories. Tony said, "Grrreeeat," this cereal popped, shredded wheat held tight, I did not like this one. I loved this one. Look at these buttons. Look at how big Tony is. Don't you just love this horse and buggy?

Yes, I would have much to tell if I had the stuff that was in that garage.

The Sandbanks. We Play Capture the Flag

Our neighborhood sandbank had two areas; one a dump, the other a hill. The dump was littered with garbage, bottles, bottle caps, broken sticks, hubcaps, paper and empty cans, including Spam (who ate that stuff?). Neighbors whose rear yards bordered it threw their garbage over the fence. On washday, they hung their clothes to dry on lines strung in those rear yards. If the air was still, the sheets did not waffle and the dump was hidden from view.

We played there. We salvaged carriage wheels for our box cart. On rainy days, we shot rats with slingshots made from tree branches. We rolled spare tires to the valley below. For walkie-talkies, we tied string between cans.

In the distance, on Valley Street, beyond the telephone and high-tension wires, an occasional truck chugged along. The fumes of rubber, like rotten eggs, streamed from the US Rubber Company. Trains rumbled at regular intervals.

The hill was different. It was dense with trees, stumps, bushes, dandelions, rocks, gravel, grass, cockleburs and trails. Its mounds of dark brown sand flowed to the valley below. Dust saturated the air on breezy, dry summer days. It was alive with rustling trees, squirrels, ticks, flies, mosquitoes, bees and flittering, small dark birds. Pines, oaks, ash and maples interrupted the skyline. Gouged by rivulets and bordered by weeds, the hill was steep enough to make me stumble. Some might think it a wasteland, but not us kids. We played in that jungle in glorious freedom away from houses, streets and cars.

We made swings from old tires tied to ropes on trees. We baked potatoes by digging a pit in the sand, lining it with rocks and crisscrossing it with logs. We lit the fire and threw in the potatoes which took hours to bake. They were delicious when we fished them out. We played games. Sure, we played games everywhere … peggy, street football, baseball, jacks, jackknives, war, cowboys, hide and seek, even hopscotch and alara … but nothing compared to the game of Capture the Flag on that hill.

The game was one of courage, cunning and speed that required nothing more than the sandbank; no equipment, no streets and no official playing field. All we needed was the space to run and the camouflage to hide. Some of us had Army canteens, belts, combat boots, jackknives and helmets. Wally even had an axe, but none of it was necessary. All we needed were PF Flyers and a flag – the red handkerchief.

Capture the Flag was the game of fun and thrills.

Captains, who chose the sides, were older, bigger, tougher, stronger and more athletic. In turn, they picked the teams, usually five or six on a side. Though small and young, I tended to go earlier because I could run fast.

Each team had its territory with a boundary line drawn in the sand. The flag stations, a few hundred yards apart and far enough to be protected out of sight, were trees with low hanging branches. The idea was to capture the opponent's flag before yours was taken and without being caught yourself.

After the picks, Ted, our captain, put his arm around me, took me aside and probably said, "Eddie, we need your speed. Don't get caught." I liked Ted, and though I felt good about being his pick, his warning concerned me.

"OK, Ted. Sure, I'm … ready."

The teams retreated to tie their flags hanging on low branches.

The flag's guard, in a zone marked in the sand by a semi-circle, came out only to capture an approaching enemy. John was our guy. John was tough, and no one could knock him off the flag.

"OK. Here's the story," said Ted. "If you get captured, you'll have to stay in their jail which will be marked by a circle near their flag, see, like ours here." He drew a circle around the goal with a stick. "You cannot get out without being tagged by one of our team. That means he got by their defenders, which ain't so easy. Get it?"

"Yeah. Yes."

"Good."

Ted took us back to the huddle where we crouched on one knee and bowed our heads like the Army guys in a movie. He continued, "Here's the story." I leaned closer, slipping, my knee scraping the gravel that tore into my thin khakis. "The fasta, bigga guys go out first. Fran, you go over the top part of the hill. Jimmy, wind your way through the middle. I'll take the low road. Remember, if you grab that flag, screw. Git yer ass back here as if your life depended on it! John, tackle anyone who gets near our flag. Yell caught! Caught! Drag him into the jail. Call for help. The only way they can get out is if someone on their team tags him." My stomach churned.

Ted turned to me. "Eddie." My eyes widened. His voice was now a hoarse whisper. "Stay back for a little bit. Watch me. I'll signal you." Fear jolted me. My mouth, already dry from the dust, was now paste. I bit my nail, licked the sweat on my lip, tightened my belt and adjusted my canteen

Ted paused, looked around and yelled through the trees, "Reaaady?"

In the distance, we heard, "Reaaady." He turned.

"OK, you guys, this is it. Go!" The first went off, then another and another, leaving John at the flag and Teddy to coach me.

"OK. Eddie. Listen. Look there." He pointed up the hill. "Circle around to the top of that hill a little behind Fran. Make your way slowly down the other side. Stay behind the trees and bushes. Crouch. Weave. Circle. Stay low. Be quiet. Watch me. Wait for my signal. See this handkerchief. I'll wave it." He wiggled a white handkerchief with blue dots. "Don't screw up!"

"OK, Ted" My mind was spinning, my vocabulary limited.

Ted scrunched his eyebrows, got closer and sneered. "No coughing, no sneezing. Sneak. Sneak in. You're small, fast. They won't notice you. Get in fast. Grab the flag and screw!"

I whispered, "You want ME to grab the flag?"

"Yes, you. The other guys will distract them. They'll never expect you to be the one to get the flag. You're a little guy. Stay quiet. Don't rustle the crows. They might give you away." He rubbed my rah-rah head.

"Crows, what crows?" I should have worn my moccasins.

"Up there."

"Yeah. OK," as I gazed at the black birds.

"OK. Go. Wait. C'mere. One more thing. Don't git captured."

"Captured? OK. Sure. No way." My heart was thumping.

Ted took off. I followed for a bit, crouching. Sounds became prominent; a screech of one branch rubbing another, small rocks tumbling, the distant train, a caw from a crow. Dam! I started my move. The world of the sand-bank was suddenly filled with dust and the muffled sound of kids running and shuffling.

Squinting into the brightness, I made my way to the top of the hill and kept my eye on Ted clawing along. The hill was a minefield of cockleburs sticking in my socks, blade grasses and musky ripe smells (my assignment took me close to the dump). But I was a commando, a member of a team, the team that wanted to win and, for sure, I did not want to screw up, or, be captured. A gust of wind blew dirt that felt like a boulder in my eye. I remember Dad saying to use only my elbow to get something out of my eye.

Not this day. I was on a mission. I rubbed. I had to see. Through tears, I made my way to the top of the hill and looked below. Ted was hiding in the bushes. He waved. I slithered and slid down toward the other goal. A rumble passed me on the right. It was Jimmy, ever bold, daring and a bit crazy as in "That kid is crazy. He'll do anything" kind of crazy steaming down the bank like a racehorse, pumping his arms, with his head lowered and his chin tucked to his neck.

I heard him bark that he would get the flag before they knew he was there.

I could not believe it. He was bounding, arms flailing, full speed down the hill. Suddenly, he slipped as he approached enemy territory. I heard the worst, "Captured. Gotcha! Gotcha, Jimmy. You're captured. Ha." Andy tackled him with a thud and had him in a bear hug, wrestling him to the ground, dragging him to their jail.

I couldn't see Ted, but he had to be pissed. He knew that if a game ended before a flag was captured, the team with the most prisoners won. Jimmy, our best guy, was in jail. Now what?

I moved across the banks with stealth. My heart was beating so loudly that I thought they could hear it. I oozed a different pungent, smellier sweat of terror. I scrunched behind a bush. An idle paper blew over from the dump. Someone tossed their garbage.

What if I was captured? I would be banned from Capture the Flag. I crawled between bushes scraping against a land mine of sharp branches that drew blood. Anything for the team. I got closer to their flag and spotted Jimmy. He waved his hand in flat, downward movements to signal quiet and for me to stay low. From the right side of the hill came Ted, running at full speed toward the enemy flag while being chased by Andy. He took out his white handkerchief and waved it toward me.

I stood and started running as fast as I could past slashing branches, huffing straight toward the flag, blowing lazily and ripe for the taking. I was no longer worried about being captured. I wanted that flag! Their goalie spotted me. "What the heck? Little Eddie? Watch him. On the other side. Get him!"

Andy turned away from Ted just as I sped past the goal, flew through the air and grabbed that red prize as a frog might snatch a bug with his tongue, spinning out of reach of Andy and their goalie. My hand curled around the flag. I was no longer worried about capture.

"Move," yelled Ted. "Go!" I did. I ran through a spider web as fast as I could, pushing downward and forward around the side of the hill and then up, up to our flag. The chase was on but too late. I saw our goalie. John screamed, "C'mon, c'mon. You got it, you got it." Huffing and puffing, I stormed past a blur of things and dropped near dead at our goal, enemy flag in hand. Ted and the rest of the guys came running. "Great job, great job. We won. We captured their flag!" They hung it alongside ours.

I gloated and stood, a hero, prouder than I had ever been. I rubbed the sweat from my eyes. They patted me. "OK. Let's get a drink. Eddie, our treat." To the corner store we went. I guzzled a Nehi orange and stood next to the guys, now one of them. We were linked by the game. It was time for a little mercurochrome and a good night's sleep.

There is a certain joy intrinsic to boys playing a game where one group succeeds and another fails. In the end, we all won because we played.

Even today, the smell of pine and maple and sometimes a little rubber takes me back to the hills and the sand banks. I think of those days. I hear a voice in the distance, "Hey, let's play Capture the Flag."

I'm ready. Let's go!

The Trolleys

Mounds of metal tethered with poles to wires that supplied the energy, the electric trolleys were masses of metallic power that glided, rumbled and wobbled along their tracks while passing rows of merchants: the tailor, shoemaker, barber, grocer, the undertaker, baker, saloon keeper, liquor store owner and fish man.

Academy Avenue was a busy neighborhood where people bustled along sidewalks and streetcars hummed along the street. Trolley tracks and overhead wires connected one end to the other.

Bulky and powerful, the trolleys pounded along the avenue, rolling their way; steel wheels on steel rails. The burning smell was from the tracks when the car came to a squealing stop. As I walked down my street toward the avenue, I heard the wheels screeching, like chalk on a blackboard. The trolley's poles swayed in the opposite direction of the streetcar. Wires looked like giant spider webs when the car stretched around the corner of Atwells Avenue's hill to the flat of Academy.

I loved to ride with Grandma on her trek to Federal Hill every Saturday. The trolley stopped one block from the end of my street. I stood on tiptoes, stretching, looking and waiting for the clanging of the bell. It was near. Its brakes thumped. I took a deep breath. The trolley was more than a ride to The Hill. The trolley was a trip out of the neighborhood.

Grandma held my hand as we boarded and passed the friendly motorman. On summer days, the trolley was crowded and hot. I sat on a wooden seat by the open window while Grandma stood, holding the leather strap, swaying to the rhythm of the ride. Elderly ladies barreled on.

On summer days, I strolled alongside the track, sometimes spotting a dead mouse, wondering what a cat or dog would look like. Or maybe half my foot. I purposely caught my shoe in the track. What if the trolley was coming? In an old movie, a femme fatal was rescued when tied to a railroad track. So what if it was a train speeding at one hundred mph and not the trolley at its maximum of fifteen. It would do just as much damage … a lost toe, foot, leg, or a life. Because I knew I could easily get my shoe out, I did it again, and again.

Sometimes Dad, in a moment of defiance and bravery when no trolley or autos were in sight would say, "Watch me drive on the tracks. Do you feel us gliding? Do you feel how smooth it is? How she slides?" He was so excited, but just as quickly as he got on the tracks, he got off with a wispy smile of mischief. I tried it with my bike, but the wheels got stuck. Of course, Dad would have disapproved if he knew what we did with the trolleys.

It was the older kids who pulled the big adventures. I might put caps in the tracks to hear the rat-a-tat-tat. That was about it. But those guys used salutes or the formidable cherry bomb which might, we thought, jolt the car off the track. We fanned out after they placed the cherry bomb, taking strategic places well out of sight. I buzzed by the bakery. That bread smelled so good but there was no time to stop. I needed to get behind the building. I wanted to watch and listen while being prepared for a getaway. This wasn't blind man's bluff or Red Rover. This was the real thing. The cherry bomb went off. A few people turned. The car rolled on its journey, unaware.

The bigger thrill was when those kids ran after the car and jumped up to pull the boom off the wire. Screech. The sound of the untethered trolley came to an abrupt powerless halt. Down two steps and around to the rear came the mumbling conductor to reattach the boom. "Damn kids!"

A road crew dug up the tracks one day and replaced them with a smooth, black street, a white line down its middle. Gone were the rumbles, clickety clacks and screeches. Gone was another neighborhood institution. Gone was that mischief.

I drove to Academy Avenue recently, visualizing the trolley following the old streets sidewalks, stores and schools, all gone. Now, so many years later, I think about those scenes. The tracks and its trolley were just another anchor among many in our neighborhood.

Wait. Was that a screech I heard?

Newspapers, a Bully and a Red Wagon

When Wally quit, the paper route was mine. Once his helper, now I was the one to assemble and deliver the papers, collect the money, cherish the tips, pay my bills and save what remained after I kept a small allowance. I added the money, school banking they called it, to a bank account I had at Old Stone Bank.

I had forty-five customers when I inherited the route. I asked the manager of the newspaper store if I could add more. "OK," Earl said. "You're sure it's not too much?"

"Nope. I can do it, Mr. B." I grew the route to seventy customers.

I hired a reliable striker, Louie, a chunky sparkplug who knew his baseball and could make the sound of a roaring crowd. We had no time to linger on stats and sounds as we buzzed along delivering that evening paper. It was all business.

I picked up the papers from the depot on Academy Avenue, packed them in my shoulder sack and off I went. In those days, the *Providence Journal* published two papers, the *Journal* and *The Evening Bulletin*. I delivered the *Bulletin* and the *Sunday Journal*.

The depot had two rooms. There were three windows in the main room. They were painted and covered with protective, crosshatched iron grates; two for the big windows and one for the small window above the door. In the center of the main room were two long wooden tables cobbled together.

Circular fans moved the stale air. In the adjacent room, Earl's office had a metal desk on which sat an old black phone in its cradle. Above the desk was a blurry mirror with a crooked diagonal crack from the left corner to the right bottom where Earl stood to adjust his tie before going to the State House where he represented his local community. There was a bathroom, I guess. Most of the time, I loved the depot with its warped floors and familiar smells of newspapers, strong ink, musty almond, dried oak and worn wood.

Earl, who always wore a shirt and tie, seemed to have the phone ever cradled in his neck. He was not much bigger than I was and, like Abe, the variety store owner, had a pasty face and balding head. He seldom smiled and looked like his next decision was about to overwhelm him.

Louie and I waited for Al, the *Journal's* driver and a goalie for the Providence Reds Hockey Team, to drop the bundles. As soon as Bill, Earl's helper, cut the wires holding the bundles, we grabbed our papers and packed the sacks.

At the tables abuzz with eager boys, I stacked my papers in my *Journal-Bulletin* bag, the one with a strap that slung over one shoulder and draped along my right side to just above the knee. I folded the papers that I had to toss.

To fold the paper, I lay it flat on the table with the front page up. Holding the right side down, I folded the left one third of the way over, creased it and then did the same with the right. The tricky part was tucking one side into the other so that it held for the throw; a side-saddle underhand toss if I was speeding by a porch or three quarter hand flick if up the stairs. Mis-folding it was trouble because it might open and float back down in two sections. I rarely missed.

Billy, a tough, strong, squinty-eyed, muscular sonofabitch, was an older kid from the neighborhood who helped Earl. He ran the shop, collated the papers, answered the phone, did the books and collected receipts. He was nasty. When he tightened his smile and looked around, I knew he was looking for a prey. When Earl was away, he tortured kids by grabbing them with a full Nelson. When he grabbed me, I had no chance. His favorite move on me was to bend my arm behind my back, pushing my hand up to the opposite scapula until I begged. "Stop. Stop." He liked that. He took pride in preying on young kids. I loathed him.

"Say uncle." I hated getting beat up, not only for the pain, but more so for the embarrassment of having the other kids feel sorry for me, or laugh. I was thinking I'd rather have the names that never hurt me rather than the sticks and stones.

"Say uncle."

"Uncle, uncle, uncle." He stopped with a smile as I was almost in tears.

"Why do you have to pick on smaller kids?"

"Because, you're here. You're a sissy and a crybaby."

"And you're a fat pig," I murmured.

"Did you say something?"

"No."

"Git outta here!"

By the time we left to deliver our papers, the place was full of wires and paper wrappers that Billy had to pick up. Ha to him.

Despite Billy, rain, snow, heat or third floors, I loved my route, though Sundays were a challenge. The paper was much larger because of the week's news summary, a magazine insert and the extra ads. I had a Radio Flyer red wagon that I filled when I arrived to the paper store after church. It was near toppling. I was alone because Louie was an altar boy. Mom wanted Dad to help.

He told her I would be fine. He was right. I was reliable in all kinds of weather. We delivered on the day of the '54 hurricane. Loyal to my customers, I refused to sell papers to people clamoring on Academy Avenue. Cars rumbled to a screeching stop. "Hey, kid, can I get a paper?" They would have paid twice as much.

"No. Sorry. They are for the customers on the route."

"C'mon. I'll give ya fifty cents for one."

"Sorry."

Collecting money was challenging but fun, especially at Christmas when I could make fifty dollars in tips. On a regular week, the daily and Sunday paper was forty-five cents. Customers flipped me a fifty-cent piece and said, "Keep the change, kid." In addition to my pay of one penny per paper per day, five cents for Sunday's paper, I averaged ten dollars a week.

I collected on Saturday mornings. Most of the customers paid on time, but it was not always easy. Sometimes I knocked and heard a shuffle but no one came to the door. I knocked again. Silence. Next week, maybe. If a month went by and I was not paid, I told Earl who took care of it. I wonder if he sent Bill.

While standing at one door, I heard the slapping of cards, the clinking of ice in glasses, the scrape of a moving chair and then, silence. After a long moment, heavy feet thumped across the kitchen, and a smiling giant in slippers opened the door. I looked up at a new customer. "Come in. Come in."

I paused, stepped gently over the threshold and entered a dark kitchen where I spotted a few people playing cards around a kitchen table. The brightest thing in the room was the stark white icebox in the corner. A puddle lay beneath. A dog barked behind a bedroom door. There was a bowl of water on the floor. I was nervous, but the nice man gave me a tip. "See you next week, kid."

"Yep. See ya." I whistled as I hustled down the stairs two at a time.

I had a coin dispenser like the trolley conductor and the ballpark guy. On collection day, I loaded up the slots for quarters, dimes, nickels and pennies. With a flick of the thumb, the change dropped into the fingers of the same hand. I was good, and fast. No one waited more than a second. I made change for a dollar with a flick, flick, slide and flick and there it was, fifty-five cents. "Fifty is good. Thanks." I slipped the nickel into my right pocket. Tips did not belong in the machine.

There were good tippers, poor tippers and some who did not tip at all.

There were those who called me a cute kid and those who never made eye contact.

There were houses with dirty stairs and houses with clean stairs. There were sounds and smells. I heard cars starting, kids playing, kids crying, people arguing, tenors practicing, dishes clanking and radios blaring. One Sunday morning, I heard a cat crying, pleading. Never having heard that sound before, I thought it was a baby behind a garage. While looking for the help of an adult on this early morning, I snuck behind the garage only to scare the cat.

I smelled cabbage, cigarettes, cigars, meatballs, old wood, new wood, sweat, dust, mold, wine, nutmeg, basil, cellars, chickens cooking and steak frying.

I remember my customers.

Dan was my closest friend, and his family was among them. His mom was a funny, loving, generous and kind woman. "Eddie, want to come for dinner tonight?" As much as she chatted, her husband, the Fire Chief, was quiet. Tall, reserved, commanding respect and as formal as a Chief might be, he rarely spoke. I was a bit in awe of him, awe bordering on fear. When we were in the same room, I did not know what to do. Once I tried to talk to no avail, so I just sat with my hands folded in my lap.

One day he spoke. "How are your Mom and Dad?" I was frozen.

"Uh, fine."

"Good." That was it. We mummed up again.

There was the man who had smooth, yellow skin that looked like tile. He had a gland problem.

There were two tenors; one who sang in the local church, the other who sang in Madison Square Garden.

There were four schoolteachers; one I had in the third grade. There was a regal priest and the man who hid when I walked by.

There was a future mayor and a future governor.

There was a college hockey player and an all-state track star. There was an all-American football player, now a school principal.

There was a person named Phil Amato who everyone called Jimmy Hagan because he liked golf. There was a man who wore a smoking jacket and held a bocchino (holder) for his cigarette.

There was a man who was wheelchair bound. I had to open his door every day to deliver his paper to him. He was alone as his wife was working. He liked to talk. I liked to run, but I didn't.

There were the parents of friends. There were girlfriends. There was our iceman who knew of Nap Lajoie, the Hall-of-Famer from Woonsocket.

There was an air force pilot. There was a firefighter. There was a nurse.

There was a tall man in a short bathrobe and slippers.

There was a short man who wore shorts.

There was a man with a twitch.

There was a cat woman with a nasal twang. There was a nasal woman with a cat twang.

There were dog lovers and dog haters. There were mean dogs and nice dogs.

There were Italians, Irish, Poles, Scots and English. There was the Scot who was a soccer star. There was the family that owned a restaurant.

There was a market and a liquor store.

The paper route taught me so much, not just how to manage a business. It connected me to my neighborhood because my customers were in it, and I was in their homes. I saw them in church, at the grocery store and on the streets.

The bullying was tough to handle, but it did not deter me. It helped me understand that not all was good, that things might be tough, and that I had to find a way to manage. I learned that there was some bad with the good I had in my life to that point, and that I could not always rely on the protection of family. I did not know it then, however. It took a while for me to understand.

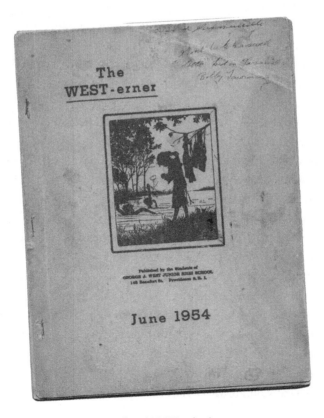

Our 1954 Yearbook

CHAPTER FOUR

JUNIOR HIGH SCHOOL

GJ West Junior High

I wonder what I would be without George J. West Junior High, one of four brick structures important to me growing up, the others being Putnam and Academy Schools and the Blessed Sacrament Church. My favorite? Well, that's easy.

It was close enough to walk and far enough to give me pause on those bitter cold winter mornings when the frost burned my face and chapped my lips. I wore my favorite hat, the toque that, even though it was not 'cool', was as warm and comforting as a good friend.

Toting my brown Kraft lunch bag and books, I walked down Wealth Avenue, took a right on Academy Avenue past the barber's and the shoemaker's and a left up one of the many hills, usually Beaufort. Miss Carroll, my favorite teacher, lived there. Beautiful, kind, elegant and engaging, she rose above classroom formality when she greeted me, smiling, "Hello, Edward. Good morning. How are you today?" never failing to drag out the Eddddwoood.

"Hi, Miss Carroll."

A splendid teacher, she was one of the many reasons I loved the school, rarely missing a day, once earning the perfect attendance award at the end-of-year ceremony.

GJW Junior High stood high in a residential neighborhood. Named in

honor of a lawyer born in Providence in 1852, a member of the school board
and active in public affairs, the school stretched along Mt. Pleasant Avenue,
spreading around the block from Beaufort Street to Roanoke with Leah
Street to the rear. It was a large, prominent red brick and granite building,
squared at each corner. Gymnasiums and playgrounds anchored the ends.
An insignia sat above the front door and at the very top was some kind of
flowery decoration too high to recognize. Elegant steps, memorialized in
our 1954 graduation picture, led to the first floor and the auditorium that
had both a stage and a balcony. Principal Cerilli's office was next to the
entrance. A taskmaster whom we admired and sometimes feared, he always
proclaimed, "West is best."

A baseball field was across the street and next to "little" Mt. Pleasant
Grammar School. Just across the street from the school, friends of my
parents' owned a striking home, a Tuscan villa which I once visited.

My first day at West was so very interesting when I realized I was
expected to go responsibly from class to class at the bell. It was the first
time I would encounter kids from different schools, neighborhoods and
towns; some bussed in from Scituate and Foster, a distance away.

Lockers lined wide wooden halls that smelled of varnish. Having the
privacy of my own locker made me feel important.

There were metal and wood shops, one gym for boys and one for girls.
There was a cafeteria where we stayed for lunch.

We started our day in homeroom with the Pledge of Allegiance and
announcements broadcast from the main office through speakers next to
which was hanging the United States flag.

Academics were strong. I had firm, dedicated teachers who prepared us
for high school: Miss Flanagan, a stout, brilliant and idiosyncratic figure
for Algebra, "Don't forget to FACTOR," clever Miss Carroll for English, testy
Miss Turbitt for History, kingly Mr. Kirby for Art and Geometry (please do
not call on me!), shaky Mr. Spinney for Woodwork, plump Mr. Lees for Art
Metal, Miss Somers for Auditorium … all very committed to their profes-
sions and their students.

The teachers seemed tough, but the principal, Guido Cerilli, set a harsh-
er tone. His values in education, dress and deportment were unyielding. He
frightened me when I witnessed two encounters with students.

Mr. Cerilli, his voice a megaphone, now nose-to-nose with a kid, barked,
"Where were you yesterday?"

"I had a cold."

1954

"A COLD?" You seem perfectly fine TODAY!"

"Sorry, Mr. Cerilli. I meant I was on the verge of a cold."

"A verge? A VERGE? I'll give you a verge. Get to my office! Get your mother in here!"

Second encounter with one of the tougher kids.

"You know that NO TAPS ARE ALLOWED on shoes," Mr. Cerilli squawked.

"My mother makes me get them to preserve the heels."

"Preserve heels. Preserve heels? You're a heel! Get ... out ... of ... here. Get to the cobblers; get them off! Bring your mother with you when you get back." The mothers came and supported Mr. Cerilli. Whew! No way was I messing with him. I stayed in the background.

It was a homogeneous student body save for those 4-H'ers who were bussed in from the periphery of Scituate and Foster, grange towns some twenty miles away. We hardly knew them as they returned to their busses after the last bell, not to be seen until the next morning, and never to be seen in our neighborhoods. We were from backgrounds that reflected a neighborhood and its cultural pattern; Italian Americans, Polish Americans, Irish Americans, etc.

I was a late bloomer, not really one of the guys and, realizing it early, I did my own thing as an early preppy surrounded by zoot-suiters. I was conscientious and crowd conscious, I was almost never mischievous. On rare moments, I lost my way when I was trying to be someone I was not.

George J. West Jr High was a world new to me, but I embraced and enjoyed it. I have a multitude of memories recounted in the stories that follow. Come with me on this chapter of my journey.

The Career Book

I wrote it in cursive with the Eversharp pen Dad gave me. My penmanship was simple with lines delineated, T's crossed one third the way up, I's dotted above, punctuation perfect. Where was this fine hand? It was in my junior high school career book.

"If you do not write a career book," growled our guidance counselor, "You WILL NOT graduate. You will REMAIN HERE another year!" Thus, for my last year at George J. West, it became a necessary, albeit final chore before my next stop at Classical High School.

Off to the library I went. My subject, Medical Doctor, was an easy pick, because one of my heroes was Dr. Fratantuono, a local practitioner friend of my father, who saved me from a trip to Boston by making a keen diagnosis. I also knew my parents would be pleased if I wrote about wanting to become a doctor.

Though I did not think it necessary at the time, I later understood why we had to write a career book. It served as a beacon, a way to learn how to do research, to introduce a learning experience, one that became a keepsake. It helped me reach a milestone in my early life. I found the book and was surprised with the memories it triggered.

The book is housed in a leather bound binder. The dark red cover has faded. Scotch taped and centered in its middle were the letters "M D" now curled at the edges. I lifted it gently from the shelf, held it and thought of the days.

The fragile pages, though still easy to read, have faded to light yellow. The edges are ragged. With caution, I rolled them back one by one.

Page one:

Medical Doctor
By
Edward Iannuccilli
Book completed on
May 4, 1954

Nine chapters follow.

Chapter I. History of Medical Doctor (three pages)

Chapter II. Successful Leaders of Medicine ... Hippocrates, Galen and Pasteur (four pages).

Chapter III. Importance of Medicine (three more).

Here is what I wrote in Chapter VIII's Compensation: *"The gross annual income is under $10,000."* Wow! (My current thought editorialized).

Here is what I wrote about Future Trends: "... *the practice of medicine has been greatly disturbed for fear that present agitation for socialized medicine or for increasing participation by the state in medical practice would result in degradation of the profession."*

I wonder where I found that paste, that disorder of words. I suspect (actually I know) I plagiarized them, even though I had references on the back pages. There were no quotation marks or footnotes.

In the rear pages were a number of pictures; a doctor with a stethoscope, a nurse, a lab machine, etc. I cut them out from magazines a local practitioner gave me. Steve, my good friend, knew I was looking for pictures, knew I was timid and one day, as we walked from school, he said, "C'mon. Let's go into that doctor's office. Maybe he has some pictures."

"We can't do that."

"Sure we can. I'll tell him it's for *my* career book." I summoned the courage and in we went in. We sat and waited. The door opened and out stepped a lanky doctor.

"Can I help you boys?"

"Yes," Steve replied. "My friend Ed is writing a career book about being a doctor, and he is looking for pictures." Steve tricked me.

Kind and reassuring, he invited us into his office and asked that we sit a moment. He gave us a few magazines and told us to cut out the pictures we needed.

"Thank you, thank you, Doctor." Thanks to Steve, I had my pictures.

As interesting and as exciting as it was to discover and pamper the book, what was more exciting and more interesting was the doctor to whom I dedicated it, Frank Fratantuono, and why.

When I was seven, I was a patient at Roger Williams Hospital, and my doctor thought lymphoma was the reason for the large nodes in my neck. He wanted to transfer me to Boston. Dad wanted another opinion, so he took me out of the hospital on Friday to the office of another physician, his friend, Dr. Frat (as we knew him), who looked into my throat, diagnosed tonsillitis and arranged a tonsillectomy for the following Monday.

GJ West Graduation Day

One day late in May 1954, I was called to Mr. Cerilli's office. I asked my homeroom teacher why, but she did not know. I was convinced I was in trouble. The word office did not sound good. I started to worry. It was the place I avoided for my three years to date.

With dread and the class looking on with compassion, I unstuck myself from the chair, left the room, trundled down the three flights of stairs and along the corridor as if molasses were stuck to my soles. Cerilli, a taskmaster, never called unless there was trouble. I knew I was done for. OK, what did I do, and how do I tell my father?

I arrived at the closed office door, wondering what lay behind it. A desk where I would spend the rest of the day under his eye? Miss F, the dreaded guidance counselor? My Dad? That's it, my Dad. He must have been called. I peered through the glass pane to see Mr. Cerilli's assistant calmly typing. She did not appear worried. Didn't she know I was summoned? I opened the door with caution. She welcomed me with a smile. A smile. Maybe it wasn't that bad. I entered.

"Have a seat. Are you Edward?" She knew something. I stood by her desk.

"Go ahead, sit." I went to the bench alongside the door, sat and rested my elbow on its arm, my head in my hand. She picked up her phone to announce my presence. I sat up, rigid.

She looked at me, tilted her head and hummed, "You can go in, Edward." Dreaded words, nicely spoken.

I opened the door and there, sitting in a maple armchair in front of Mr. Cerilli, who was sitting behind his desk and smiling, was Dr. Fratantuono. My goodness, my doctor! What was going on? Mr. Cerilli stood. "He's bigger and broader than I realized," I thought.

Dr. Frat sat a moment. Everyone had a way of taking their time like the teacher, the secretary and now Dr. Frat. He finally stood and extended his hand. I did not remember him as being so big. Maybe it was the small office.

He took a step forward. I shook his hand. Tall, stately, he bent down, looked over his wireless glasses with squinting eyes, a jolly red face and a soft expression and said, "Hi, Edward." He was so nice, so formal. He took off his glasses and polished them. In the presence of these two giants, I stood motionless, hands by my side.

"Please sit, Edward." I inched back into a chair. "The good doctor came in today and asked to see you. The doctor is here to talk to you about your career book." Mr. Cerilli, though formal, was now mellow.

"My book?"

"Yes, Edward," Dr. Frat said. He had the book open to the dedication page where I had written:

This book is dedicated to Dr. Frank Fratantuono, who, through his successful work in this occupation has helped me to try and follow in his footsteps.

His hand caressed the page. "I am honored that you dedicated your book to me, and even more thrilled that you want to be a doctor. What prompted this honor?" I told him the lymphoma story. "Well, well. I had forgotten that. Wasn't your Dad wise to get another opinion?" I took a deep breath. Should I have dedicated the book to Dad?

Dr. Frat handed me a small box wrapped in white paper and tied with a thin blue ribbon. An envelope was taped to it. "You can open the note when you get home, but I'd like you to open the box now if you would."

I slid off the ribbon, carefully tore the paper and opened the box. It had the word Cross on the cover. It was a gold Cross ballpoint pen engraved with my name; the first among many I was to receive over the years. I still have it.

"Thank you, Dr. Frat. Thank you," I gulped. I looked at Mr. Cerilli. "May I leave now?"

"Yes, sure, Edward, sure, good job." They both shook my hand.

"Thank you."

"No, thank you, Edward." He rested his hand on my shoulder.

I hurried home at day's end. "Look at this, Dad, Mom. Dr. Frat came to the school with it. I met him in Mr. Cerilli's office." I showed them the pen. I opened the card slowly, took out the note and read what he wrote in tall letters slanted to the right as if blown by the wind. (I found the note tucked in the book for these many years). He wrote:

Edward,

It was indeed a thrill to read your career book, and it was a great honor to have you dedicate it to me. This is an example of a truly great reward, and makes material gains fade into darkness. I trust that God will give me the strength, and that He gives you the guidance to fulfill your ambition. Thank you.

F.D. Fratantuono, M.D. 7/1/54

"Oh, Edward, that's wonderful," effused Mom.

"Good job, Ed." Dad called me Ed when he was pleased. The buttons near exploded off his shirt.

There is a trove of things one may keep from the past. I have kept a lot, though I wonder what of it should remain and for how long? What will my children do with the stuff when I am gone? Will those things so personal fade along with me into darkness? Who will care that I have a career book, a pen and a note?

What is important? What do we leave for the next generations, understanding that things we accumulate can choke a landfill? I have no answer.

I am delighted, overjoyed, that I kept this career book. It tells the story of a future, a dream fulfilled. It was a turning point in my life, one that I treasure because it reminds me of so many who gave me the strength and direction to act upon a dream.

I decided what I wanted to be in junior high school, and there my journey started.

The Guidance Counselor Gets Me on My March for Pizza

Now and again, opportunity results in bad decisions. One day, I had a smoldering desire for pizza from DeLuise's Bakery across the ball field, beyond the elementary school and Chalkstone Avenue. DeLuise's was the best place for pastry, pies and strip pizza; a neighborhood destination of smells, flavors and tastes. The Napoleons and sfogliatelle were amazing, but nothing beat the strip pizza. I could taste it from afar, and afar I was when the idea hit.

I skipped out before lunch break, scooting across the ball field for the warm, soft, savory, baked bread, crisp on the bottom and smeared above with layers of tomato sauce. I looked at my Dick Tracy watch. I had time to get back before the other students went to lunch.

The ball field was a stretch of infield dirt and outfield grass. A high chain-link fence protected the homes in left field. Rabid, I marched along, picking up the pace by third base, second base and right field toward center, kicking dust while looking over my shoulder. I had never done anything like this. Once I wanted to be a zoot-suiter, so I tried the suede shoe, fourteen inch pegged pants, turned up collar, long hair, ducks-ass look, but that lasted for a week. Not for me. I was a blue shirt, white bucks, baggy khaki pants, wavy haired predictable kid. To do something out of the ordinary, like changing my wardrobe or leaving school early for pizza was a little frightening, but I was on my way, and there was no turning back.

Money from my paper route was jingling in my pocket. I crossed the street to the bakery and opened the door to the overwhelming aroma of pizza. I strolled to the counter. The strips were stacked neatly in a tray on top, wax paper separating the oily layers. Ah, the pizza; ten cents a slice.

"May I help you, son?"

I looked around. "Yes. I would like two slices of pizza. Can you make one of them an end?"

"Sure. Aren't you out on lunch break a little early?"

George J. West Boys

"Uh yeh, I guess." She wrapped the pieces in wax paper, put them in a bag and handed it to me. I gave her the twenty cents, spun around, walked out the door and crossed the street. The oil, seeping through the bag, was a calling card.

Once across the street, I opened the bag, reached in and pulled out the end piece, peeling away the wax paper after each bite. I devoured it, crunching the corners while savoring the taste of the tomatoes. Oil slipped down my chin. I wiped it with my sleeve. I folded the second piece in its wax paper, put it in the bag and carried it in my other hand. I licked the oil from my fingers and began my march back across the field thinking that by the time I got to second base, I would be ready for the remaining piece. Still no one had been dismissed for lunch.

As I approached second base, I looked up to see her, the guidance counselor, an imperial, matriarchal hulk of a woman, standing in the school doorway, hands on hips. I could not see her face, but I knew she was wearing a scowl. I felt her steely eyes boring through me from afar.

I stopped, turned toward right field took a step, started, turned back, turned to left field, took a step and stopped, again. She waved. Head down, I shuffled my way across the infield, dragging my feet in the dust. I was done for.

After an eternity, I approached her. She filled the door's space. "What's this about?' she barked. "Why are you out while NO ONE HAS BEEN DISMISSED? And what's that in your hand?"

"Uh, not sure." I looked at my hand. "Pizza?"

"Come with me." I blundered along, following her heavy heels that clicked along the corridor. By this time, the kids were getting out of class. They stopped. There was nowhere for me to hide the bag. My pocket could never handle the bag and the oil. They snickered. They knew. Crowd conscious and humiliated, I trailed her down the corridor to her office like a shamed puppy, passing other kids now gliding along on their way to lunch. Now I tried to pocket the bag to no avail. She stopped. She turned. I stopped. She motioned me into her office and told me to sit.

I passed by her as she stood at the door to her inner sanctum. Impatient, indignant, she was eyeing my pizza with calculated appraisal, one eye half closed, her lip turned up. Maybe she wanted a bite. That's it. I'll give it to her. She could take it to the teacher's lunchroom. What if I offered the slice in return for a pardon?

She sat behind her desk. I avoided eye contact as I slouched in the hard chair alongside her desk. She sat miles above, staring over her glasses.

"Sit up. Good posture. What is this about?"

"I was hungry, so I went for pizza." I sat up and held the pizza low beside the chair as a trickle of oil slithered down my fingers.

"You know this is unacceptable."

"Yes, I do."

With a nefarious glare and an arthritic curl of her hand, she picked up a fat pen. "What do you think I should do? I could call your parents, you know. Even worse, I can get the Principal."

"I don't know."

She paused, solemn, staring at me, her granite chin tilted slightly upward. "OK. Get out of here." I bolted out of the chair. "Don't let it happen again. And, by the way, get rid of that pizza."

Get rid of the pizza!? Curses, the final blow, the worst sentence of all. I tossed the greasy bag into the bucket near the door and wiped my hand on my khaki pants again. "Yes, Miss F," I replied, one foot out the door, the bucket pizza not easily forgotten.

Who Took My Pills

Our science teacher was also our homeroom teacher. With her, we started, and ended each day. Homeroom teachers were sitters; taking attendance and propping us up for the long day. They were not as strict as the classroom teachers. Miss S was firm, serious, poised and organized. She placed her lunch in the same place on the right front side of her oak desk every day.

At the bell just before noon, we returned to home room, retrieved our lunch bags and waited for the next bell. Steve had placed his lunch bag on Miss S's desk because he had forgotten something in his locker. We liked Miss S, and we wanted to give her a gift for her up-coming birthday, so we asked her to leave the room for a moment. While she was out, Steve, upon his return, grabbed a lunch off her desk. He was not aware that it was hers.

Hungry, he opened the bag and saw two small packets wrapped in foil. Thinking that it was a bit unusual because his mother always used wax paper, he opened the larger of the two; a dry sandwich with a little piece of meat. He put it aside and opened the smaller package. In it were what looked like two red M&M'S. Without thinking why his mother might give him only two, he popped them into his mouth.

"Ugh. Awful. What the hell was that? What is my mother thinking? Half a dry sandwich and two candies?" He spit them into the trash. That's when he looked up to see another bag on the desk – oops. He figured it out. He had Miss S's lunch. So he snatched his bag just as the bell rang for lunch period and scooted, blurting as he bounded down the stairs, "C'mon, let's scram."

He stopped half way. "I had Miss S's lunch. I grabbed it without thinking. How does she survive with such a little lunch, half a sandwich? Why would someone take only two or three M&M'S for dessert?" He paused. "Oh my God! I'll bet these red things weren't M&M'S but pills. Geez, I hope she doesn't die. I should never'uv eaten lunch in the room. What the heck was I thinkin? I never do that."

At a silly pitch, we laughed, sort of, though it wasn't that funny. "Yeah," we said, "We hope she doesn't die. Or something like that." We scrambled down the stairs.

George J. West Girls

Steve stood back. We stopped. He looked at us. We looked at him. " You guys are my friends and ya gotta keep this quiet right, or I'll be screwed, in a messa trouble."

"OK, Steve. You got it. We gotta keep quiet or you'll be in trouble. You bet. Yep. We'll do it."

Miss S returned to the room. Perplexed, she looked at her desk. "What happened to my lunch? My pills!"

After lunch, Bob and I went to play wall ball as Steve went to talk to some friends. Miss F, the rough and tough guidance counselor, stopped us and guided us to her office for a chat.

We returned to homeroom before going to afternoon classes. As we sat, the door opened and in came both teachers. The room quieted.

The guidance counselor rarely came to our room. Miss F wore dollops of red rouge that accentuated her pallor. Sneering and wearing a deep frown, she spoke slowly and with a firm, raspy voice that sounded like she was at the bottom of a well, "OK. Some. One. Took. Miss S's la-unch. I neeeddd to knoowww WHO did, it, be-cause she … had … her … pills … in … there. And she NEEDSHERPILLS!!" Grrr.…

"Who took my pills?" Miss S asked, clasping her shaking hands at her waist with an air of desperation. Her pallor matched the wall.

The class, sitting like trained seals in a row and sporting wide-eyed expressions of "We know who," turned to look at Steve. How did they know? Well, Bob and I somehow let his secret out, or something like that. And I guess we told some classmates. "OK, Miss F barked, "Where are her pills? She needs them. Steven."

"Uhhh, in the trash where I spit them."

"GET THEM."

Steve, awkward, apologetic and humiliated in front of the class, fished the partially mashed pills out and handed them over. He then left with the scowling counsellor and spent the day in her office. When school ended, we met. We looked down as he barked, "You guys are my friends and you promised. You promised not to tell!" He was annoyed, as annoyed as this happy kid could ever be. Did I detect a smile?

"What did ya tell?" he begged.

"Nothing, nothing. We never said what happened. We never told her you had Miss Sherman's lunch, never said your name."

"Then, how the heck did she know?"

"Well, she asked us who did it. We told her we didn't know. No way, Steve. No way. But she would not stop. She kept buggin' us, askin' over 'n over. We don't know, we replied, over 'n over. That was good, huh?"

"Yeah," I guess," said Steve. "So what happened?"

"Miss F hounded us."

Miss F said, "OK, let me ask you this," she continued as she hovered over us with her hands on her healthy hips, upper lip quivering and steam coming from her flared nostrils. "If you HAD TO GUESS *who* might do such a terrible thing, who would you say?"

Stammering, we replied, "J … j, just a guess, Miss F, j, just a guess. But uh, why, uh, Steve. Steve. Yeah, that's it. Stevie. Or somethin' like that. Guess was bad, huh Steve?"

"That's what you guys said? You bet it was bad! Thanks a lot. Thanks.

But ya know what? You guys're still my friends. Ya know why? They're gonna put me in the un-graded room for a week, and I won't have to do anything. And I get two lunch periods every day! I'm looking forward to it. So I forgive you."

'Thanks, Steve." Good friends we remained.

The Cafeteria and the Game

Inside a cafeteria lives a smell. Smells stir memories. Not long ago, I toured my junior high school and came to the cafeteria. Its musty, steamy, stale smells hovering along the low ceilings conjured up recollections of lunch hour. With blindfolds, I would recognize the place.

The cafeteria was in a basement that also housed the art metal and woodworking shops across the corridor. The "caf" had two doors opening on either side. There were rows of tables interspersed among supporting metal poles. Florescent lights tinged yellow made everyone and everything seem waxy.

At the bell, we rushed from our classrooms, raced to our lockers, grabbed our lunches, scurried down the stairs and tumbled into our places, boys to one side, girls to the other. We tossed our lunch bags on the tables and jockeyed into the food line to buy a carton of milk. It was noisy and hectic, with kids bounding about, while those with trays in hand, stood in line along a steel rail that defined the 'kitchen' where the ladies served lunch. That area smelled of boiling cabbage and wet bread.

At the beginning of the line was a stack of trays adjacent to the steaming bins of food. Behind the bins were busy, paper-hatted women dressed in pale pink, serving. Behind the servers was the kitchen where the smells originated. At the end of the parade was another woman in pink sitting at a cash register.

I rarely stood in the food line. I carried my lunch except on pizza days. Yes, sometimes even then.

Mom made me a baloney sandwich with French's mustard on Tip-Top or Wonder Bread, wrapped in wax paper and put it in a Kraft brown bag. The tangy mustard gave the bland baloney a kick. On occasion, she made a potato and egg omelet sandwich. The snack, however, was the highlight; Hostess Twinkies or a Devil Dog. As we ate, we chatted about the Red Sox, Yankees, pro football, Otto Graham, Y. A. Tittle, Dante Lavelle, Jim Brown, radio shows like *Boston Blackie, The Phantom* or *The Shadow*. On Wednesdays, we repeated Milton Berle's jokes from his Tuesday night show. On Fridays, we spoke of watching *The Hopalong Cassidy Show* that evening. We discussed what we would do after school.

We looked to the other side of the room to see if the girls were watching. They never were. There was Maryann flipping her pony tail as she chatted. I played a kissing game with her once, but she had to teach me how to kiss. I imagined her walking over to me to say, "Hi" in front of the other boys, but that never happened. In fact, nothing like that ever happened to me.

I returned to cafeteria chat and probably said something like, "Do you think Maryann likes me?"

"How should we know?"

"She asked me to go to the movies."

"Ya think that's a clue? Did you say yes?"

"I don't know," milk from the straw snapped out and strafed Steve. He looked at his shirt.

"How can you not know if you said yes or not?"

"I don't know."

Teachers stood by to keep the noise down to a soft roar. Lunch was quick. Recess followed. I tossed down the milk and bolted to the schoolyard, a blacktopped area to the rear of the school where we played baseball using our fists for a bat.

The rules were the same, except there was no pitcher and no one struck out. Why? Because we threw a Spaldeen to ourselves and struck it with a closed fist, trying to place it in the field or hit the wall of the school. The bigger kids could toss the ball straight up and take a roundhouse overhand swing from the hip to launch the missile to hit the wall. Home runs were rare as a hard hit ball off the wall might ricochet to the second baseman in the small yard.

I never could hit the wall. So, I threw the ball sideways, swinging my arm horizontally, trying to sneak a grounder between the fielders. One day, I shuffled to the plate, took the Spaldeen in hand, tossed it up a little way, took my sideways swing and hit it between the fielders to reach first base, a rarity. I was thrilled.

As the next batter came to the plate, I leaned off first to get a lead and guess what! The first baseman tagged me. I was stymied by the hidden ball trick and got picked off! Picked off! No one should be picked off, least of all by the hidden ball trick in a school yard! I was stunned and stood motionless, red-faced, as embarrassed as if my pants had fallen. "Damn it," someone yelled.

I lost all hope. With uneasy tears in my eyes, I took off as fast as I could and headed for, yep, you guessed it, the cafeteria. I knew no one would be there. It was now dark. I sat in a chair in the corner and rested my elbows on the table with my head between my hands. A woman in pink came from the kitchen. "Anything wrong, son?"

"No. I'm fine." Thinking that my baseball career might be over, I was comforted by the solace of the cafeteria. "Maybe I'll stay here for the rest of the day," I thought.

I was surprised by her soft voice. "We'll be closing the doors shortly."

The day I took the tour, I saw that the lighting had not changed, the food line was the same, and the tables were in their same places.

I pictured the teachers, heard the dishes clanging, the cash register ringing, shoes tapping, chairs tumbling and the din of kids talking, shouting, whistling and laughing. I wished I had a carton of milk, a Devil Dog and was again there to gaze at the girls.

I saw myself sitting at that corner table after that game.

The Band Concert

By now, you all know how much I wanted to play the drums; not just play, but play like Gene Krupa. My passion was palpable. Since I had no drums, I played on the desk, the porch or the bedpost with sticks alone. At West, I played cymbals and bass drum because Johnny was so much better on the snare, my ultimate desire. One day, my time came.

I was surprised when Mr. Falciglia asked me to play snare for one of the songs at the upcoming concert. I was to play Cheery Berry Bim; not Krupa, but a start.

"Mom, Dad, I'm finally going to play the drums in a concert. On stage. Next Wednesday."

"That's great, Edward. What song?" asked Mom.

"Cheery Berry Bin."

"I love that song. Da, da, da, da, da, da, da, da ... " Mom loved to sing. She once played the piano.

The day came. The numbers before mine were a blur and in the way of my debut. I was focused on, and tapping, Cherry Berry Bim. During rehearsal, Mr. Falciglia told us to watch his baton, follow the beat. Ha-rum, thum, thum, thum. Ha-rum, thum, thum, thum. I asked if I could do a drum roll, but was quickly thwarted. I thought of flicking the sticks and sneaking the roll in.

For the early tunes, I played the bass drum. Johnny was playing snare, bass and standing cymbal. Finally, Mr. Falciglia waved his hand in a sweeping motion. My turn. Band members moved to different positions. I switched with Johnny, sat, adjusted the seat, made sure my foot reached the pedal, grabbed the sticks, tilted the snare and waited … trembling.

"Ready, set," said Mr. Falciglia in a hushed voice. He raised both hands, the baton in one.

Just then, I looked up at the balcony and there was my mother. What was she doing there? She had never been to a concert. Why would she? She worked. I never had a solo. She looked beautiful sitting there in the last row, kinda snuck in so I wouldn't know she was there. As I remember, she was wearing a tan, flowered dress and a wide brimmed hat. She was sitting alone. My trembling stopped.

I heard tapping and looked up to see Mr. Falciglia pattering the baton on his stand. He was glaring at me. Was he not happy about something? Oh, yeah, sure. I got it. I was supposed to start the tune with a boom on the bass and a rat-a-tat on the snare. The band was to follow. No wonder he was annoyed at my day dreaming.

Foot on the pedal, sticks in hand, I was now ready. He raised his baton and down it came. Bass … boom, snare … tap, tap, bass … boom … snare … tap, tap … Cheery Berry Bin … ha-rum, thum, thum, thum. I was beating the bass drum with a foot pedal rather than wielding a mallet with my hand. The beat was crisp, a trum rather than a thrum. I liked it. I really liked it. It rattled my leg. The band followed. Me!

Da, da, da, da da, boom, tap, tap, tap – da, da, da, da, boom, tap, tap, tap. Not exciting but necessary. I remember his words, "You are the important part of the band. You keep the beat. They follow."

It was not the rhythm of Benny Goodman's "Sing, Sing, Sing" nor did it require a drum roll, only boom, tap, tap, tap, boom, tap, tap, tap.

I never missed a beat. I didn't have to read music. All I needed was his baton. I thought it was going so well that on one of the snare thums, I tried a roll … rrrr-thrumppp. Mr. Falciglia glared and pointed his baton at me. Foiled, but it was worth it.

The song was over. Mr. Falciglia was smiling and whispered, "Good,

good." I heard clapping. I looked up at the balcony. Mom was clapping.

I liked it. Another wave by Mr. Falciglia and I returned to the bass drum.

When the concert ended, I met Mom in the lobby. "Edward, that was great."

"Mom. I didn't know you were coming. How did you get here?"

"I walked." She walked to school, just like I did every morning. She walked to come see me play. She took a day out of work.

"Thanks, Mom." That's about the best I could do for emotion. There was no way I was going to hug or kiss her, even though she tried an athletic extension.

"Edward, you were wonderful. I loved it. Would you believe I love you?" She always said that.

"Yeah, yeah. I gotta go. Thanks. See ya later." I skipped off.

What a day.

My Favorite Teacher

Recently, I was thumbing through a book of poetry and came across Walt Whitman's *O Captain! My Captain.* Reflexively, I recited the first stanza, the one my junior high teacher had us memorize so many years ago. She introduced me to poetry.

Miss Carroll was lovely, joyful and relaxed; at home in her profession. She wore tailored clothes and dark shoes with short heels. Dark rimmed glasses complemented her speckled silver hair. She used a hint of makeup, a wisp of lipstick, had a way of squinting her ice blue eyes when she was not satisfied, not because there was a problem, but because she wanted us to do better, work harder, think more and, above all, learn.

Her crinkled face and narrow eyes were a look of concern that we were not thinking, that we should have known something had we paid attention; that we should take advantage of the opportunities. I wanted to listen to learn.

Miss Carroll introduced something new and different every day.

To start each class, she read inspirational quotes from Fr. Keller's book. Sure, he was a Catholic, a Christopher. No matter. She did not intend to make converts. She was teaching, not preaching. She planted a good thought in our heads to start her class on a positive note.

"How would you describe eternity?" she asked one day. She removed her glasses with one hand and placed the other on the back of her neck, just above the white collar of her navy-blue dress. We sat quietly. She answered her own question. "Eternity is longer than forever. If you counted every grain of sand on every beach in the entire world, you would not get to the number. Eternity is longer than that."

Graduation Day

She asked us to write a story about someone from a foreign country. I was proud to write about someone from Sweden. Pleased with it, I titled it *"The Sweden."*

"Did you mean *The Swede*, Edward?" as, smiling, she handed me the paper.

"Yes, Miss Carroll. I think I did."

Another day, she read *Casey at the Bat*. I listened intently, captured by the legend, not taking my eyes off her for a moment, identifying with Casey and waiting for his heroics. She read with emotion, much like a Broadway actor. When she read the ending,

> *The sneer is gone from Casey's lip, his teeth are clenched in hate;*
> *He pounds with cruel violence his bat upon the plate.*
> *And now the pitcher holds the ball, and now he lets it go,*
> *And now the air is shattered by the force of Casey's blow.*
> *Oh, somewhere in this favored land the sun is shining bright;*
> *The band is playing somewhere, and somewhere hearts are light,*
> *And somewhere men are laughing, and somewhere children shout;*
> *But there is no joy in Mudville – mighty Casey has struck out.*

"Mighty Casey has struck out," I blurted. "He struck out!"

She glanced at me with a warm, patient smile and whispered. "Yes, Edward, he struck out. He struck out. That's all. Stay calm." Perhaps that was her way of introducing failure and having us learn to accept it.

She had us memorize noteworthy parts of poems. I found it difficult because I could not visualize it. I had little appetite for it, not sure why she made us commit to memory. I am pleased now that she did, because when I read one of those poems today, I connect with the days when learning was so extraordinary. I can recite those passages.

Kilmer's

> *"I think that I shall never see*
> *A poem as lovely as a tree ... "*

And Whitman's ...

> *O Captain! My Captain! Our fearful trip is done,*
> *The ship has weathered every rack, the prize we sought is won,*
> *The port is near, the bells I hear, the people all exulting,*
> *While follow eyes the steady keel, the vessel grim and daring;*
> *But O heart! Heart! Heart!*
> *O bleeding drops of red,*
> *Where on the deck my Captain lies,*
> *Fallen cold and dead.*

"You know, class, Whitman was writing about his hero. Who do you think it might be?" No response. "If you read further and think about it, you may realize that Whitman was writing about his and everyone's hero, President Lincoln. Look at the part." She pointed out the lines and read softly,

My Captain does not answer, his lips are pale and still:
My father does not feel my arm, he has no pulse nor will:
The ship is anchored safe and sound, its voyage closed and done:
From fearful trip, the victor ship, comes in with object won:
Exult O shores, and ring, O bells!
But I with mournful tread
Walk the decks my Captain lies,
Fallen cold and dead.

"He was writing about President Lincoln's assassination."
We read Sea Fever by Masefield.

I must go down to the seas again, to the lonely sea and the sky,
And all I ask is a tall ship and a star to steer her by.

When she read Whittier's poem, Barbara Frietchie, the lines

"Shoot if you must this old gray head
But spare your country's flag," she said.

fixed Miss Carroll's lovely gray hair in my mind. The poems were rhythmi-
cal, light, understandable and repeatable.

One day, Miss Carroll disappointed me. Nick, Al and I told the class that
we were going to a difficult college prep high school, Classical. She asked
the class if they thought I would do well at that "very difficult school."

"No," they said at her prompt. I was devastated, but I went anyway
and succeeded. Some years later when I was a medical student, I met
Miss Carroll.

"Hi, Miss Carroll. Do you remember me?"

"Yes, Edward, I do."

"Do you remember suggesting that I might have difficulty at Classical?"

"No, I do not."

With a gentle voice, I stumbled, "Well … you … did, but you were
wrong. I did well, and I am now a medical student."

"Well, at times we teachers are wrong, Edward, and I apologize."
She smiled. She was, and always had been, my favorite. Her response was
predictable, humble, kind once more. I was restored. At that moment, she
became my educator again, and I remembered all those exceptional things
she did to make me a good student, good enough to be successful,
to achieve.

"Thank you, Miss Carroll. It is so nice to see you. I loved your English class. You were the best."

"Thank you, Edward."

Off I went, glancing over my shoulder. I wondered why she never married. She was smart and attractive. There is more to the story.

My best friend in high school lost his mother. His Dad, a prominent lawyer, was a widower. Later in his life, he met Miss Carroll and married her.

I met her again years later. She was now my patient. "Mrs. M, do you remember the day you read *Casey at the Bat?*" And that you had us memorize poems.

"I do, Doctor. Yes, I do."

"Thank you for that."

"You're welcome."

What makes a teacher great? How about love for her profession, love for students, scholarly wit, humor, common sense, passion, compassion, patience and kindness. A touch of spirituality.

Miss Carroll had them. How lucky we were.

> *"I think that I shall never see*
> *A poem as lovely as a tree ... "*

Gym Teachers, Communism and a Broken Thumb

Whistles dangling around their necks, our gym teachers were proper men who laughed rarely, disciplined regularly and taught conscientiously.

Mr. D patrolled the floor with a stern face, black hair combed straight back and the ends of his eyebrows turned up. A rare smile was a thin line curved in a sharp crescent below his nose that grew dark hairs from the inside out. He wore the clothes of a gym instructor; gray shirt, black shoes, black belt and black pants. He was a disciplinarian who taught the horse, the rings, the mats, the knotted rope climb and the dangers of Communism. Yes, the dangers of Communism.

If a kid needed discipline, he sent him not to the principal's office but to stand in front of the locker room doors. With a guttural and nasal twang and a wooden voice, he barked, "Sonnn, guarrrd the locker room doors. Do ... not ... let ... any ... comm-u-nists... in!" His voice rendered motionless this student who was afraid to do something, anything wrong.

We may have heard of the dangers of communism, but we never feared that communists would get into the locker room. It was below street level, and someone was always "guarding" it. How would WE know what a communist looked like? We knew he had to be joking. Communists? Here?

Mr. P was another stern teacher. He was Norm, a quirky character who filled the air with unending, tedious stories. He taught health education. He loved to talk and had a story for everything, from health and sports to WWII. Norm was tall, had pale blond-white hair, wore tan-rimmed glasses that slid down his nose of his ruddy, cheery face. When he was annoyed, the smile stayed but with a twist. He wore the same clothes every day. When he coached our away basketball games, he arrived wearing a tattered gray soft hat with a rim of sweat and an old, gray, faded, frayed top coat with stains running alongside the black buttons.

One of the fathers said, "Look at the guy. He's been wearing those things since WWII. The hat. The topcoat. He must be kidding." We bent in a spasms of uncontainable laughter; the kind when you don't want someone to know it's about him, the kind that gets worse and more dynamic because you tried to hold it back.

"Anything wrong, fellas?" he asked.

"No, Mr. P" Brrarphhph.

Norm patrolled our games of touch football on the school's fields.

Bobby threw a long pass that I caught for a touchdown one day. Mr. P said, "Iannuccilli's team scores again." I loved it. That's why I loved him. He noticed what we did and gave us credit. He gave me a chance to play on the basketball and baseball teams.

He was my first coach. Though I was small and not as skilled as the older kids, he made me a part of the team. He chose me as the starting second baseman on the baseball team. "OK, Iannuccilli, here's your chance. Get out there."

Early in the first game, I took a throw from the catcher. The runner slammed his foot into my gloved hand, snapping it back and causing so much pain that I had to come out of the game. Dad took me to the emergency room. I had broken my thumb. The doctor splinted it and wrapped it with enough gauze to make me an obvious warrior.

The next day, I saw Mr. P. "Eddie, what happened?"

I pointed. "Thumb. Broken. Out. For the season."

"That's too bad." He cared.

Those gym teachers made an impression, not because they were idiosyncratic and quirky, but because they were professionals, teaching exercise, skill, health, understanding, and discipline. I needed someone to encourage me, test me, give me the answers and help me grow. They did it.

I never saw a communist, I broke my thumb, I sat out the season. I was disappointed. I was growing up.

We Visit George J. West

After sixty years, a small group of graduates thought we should revisit the old school. We meet regularly for lunch. We reminisce, laugh and have fun.

Following one of the luncheons, we arranged to tour the school with the assistant principal, an enthusiastic, accommodating lady appreciative of our fondness for West.

We entered through the front doors of the red brick behemoth and gathered at the main entrance, next to our former principal Cerilli's office. We strolled down the lobby to the portrait of the school's benefactor, George J. West, a well-respected lawyer, educator and member of the school board in the early 1900's. The school was built in 1916.

It was as large as we recalled. It is no longer a junior high, but rather a middle school for almost 900 children.

We were surprised and pleased that it had held up so well. The auditorium, where we attended assemblies, danced, sang, acted, watched movies, played music and graduated, changed little. It had a balcony, projection booth, stage with curtains and a functioning sound system.

I could hear us belting out the words to the West fight song at music assembly ...

> *Forward on for George West School*
> *And let the skies above you know ...*
> *Fight, fight, fight for George West School*
> *And let the rousing trumpets blow ...*

From the auditorium, we went to the gym and then to the cafeteria. The lingering smells of meals long ago hovered yet. We visited the art room, the woodworking and art metal shop rooms and the classrooms, the last stop our home room, 310. The smell of wood, chalk, pencils, erasers and metal rekindled our memories even more.

We paused to reflect. A wave of emotion ran through me. The desks looked the same. The windows were spacious and light poured in. There was one thing missing, Miss S's desk. In its place was an easel.

Carolyn remembered the seating plan, Bill remembered the work station and Steve remembered the wayward lunch. I remembered the new teacher who came when Miss S retired.

As we exited to stroll the corridor, we looked in the empty lockers hoping, I guess, to find something we may have scrawled or left behind. We opened the doors to the stairwell, our mind's eye watching the past as we bounded two stairs at a time. This day we walked down carefully, one at a time.

Back to the main corridor. George J. West looked proud. He should be. We are.

We're headed right
With red and white
At George West Junior High …

CHAPTER FIVE

DAYS AT THE BEACH

The Beach House

After years of summer Sunday caravans, I was delighted when for the month of July, 1952, my parents rented a cottage at the Narragansett shore with my aunt, uncle and cousins. I was thirteen; we would be living across the street from the beach … staying overnight … many overnights. No riding in the hot car for hours. No packing. No bathing suit blues. No Sterno. No tiring trip home in traffic.

It was not the first house our family had rented in Narragansett. When I was a toddler, my family rented for a week; my only memories gleaned from pictures like the one where I was holding grandfather's hand, he in his bathrobe and me in my bathing suit, our cottage in the rear. I was a prince, the first and only grandchild so far.

This year was different. On those scorching July days spent on the beach, we watched breaking waves, fleets of wispy clouds looking down on us, sunrises, sunsets and the Block Island ferry on the distant horizon, predictably passing by at eleven and returning at five, cutting a white line in the dark water. We could set our clocks by it.

The house was a white, speckled cinder block cottage hunkered a touch away from its identical mate. Next to that was a small cottage, and next to that a mansion surrounded by a beach-gray ten foot fence.

Inside the cottage, a paper-thin knotty pine wall barely touching the

crest of the roof divided the cottage into two living spaces. It smelled of
coffee, pine, salt air and warm water with a touch of bleach. Centered at the
entrance by the screen door was the only bathroom; one bathroom, four
adults, five kids and no indoor shower. A spiral of flypaper hung above the
entrance.

Each side had two rooms. In the kitchen was an ice box, a spindly wood-
en table covered with a flowery oilcloth where we played checkers, war and
Monopoly and a cot. Metal folding chairs for visitors rested against a wall.
On the other side of the wall was a bedroom with two double beds near
touching. At night, Uncle's snoring poured over the "separating" wall into
our bedroom. On some evenings, two fog horns were synchronized ... his
and the Point Judith Light.

The springs in the wobbly mattresses were spiky and hurt. I never could
get all of the sand out of the bed. On the windowsill next to my bed, I stored
my beach treasures; a smooth black stone, a dry starfish, a conch shell that
held the ocean's roar, periwinkle shells, punk, a deck of Bicycle cards and a
gimp bracelet. Under the bed were the sparklers for the 4th.

Up the road were Adams' Store, Aunt Carrie's, Cozy Corner Grille, the
Boy's Police Camp and the beach concession stand that sold French fries
floating in white vinegar.

We woke to the shining sun and the smell of bacon, eggs and toast.
Morning whitecaps were pink from the sun's reflection. We went from
pajamas to bathing suits, had breakfast and strolled across the tarred street
to the beach, barefoot, with towels draped around our necks. On Sundays
and holidays, we strutted across the street between lines of overheating cars
creeping to the shore after their ride from the city. And they had to pack
and drive back!

"Watch the traffic. Careful in the water. Don't go too far. Tell the lifeguard you're there. We'll be right over." Moms being Moms.

"See ya," we barked as we headed to the beach – a long stretch of sand
that started at the rocks to our left and ended at Lido Beach to our right.
We fiddled at water's edge, skimmed rocks, rode the waves, buried each
other and dug holes to China.

The water was magic, but I was not quick to dive. The cold hurt my
ankles. I stopped, wet my hands, then my arms, crouched, wet my shoulders
and waited for the next wave, rising on tiptoes to keep the cold from my
crotch. With several puffs, I dove, rose quickly and gasped. "There, I did it."

We flew kites, made sand castles, collected shells, rocks, starfish and periwinkles. We swam, snorkeled, swam, caught crabs, swam, rode the waves, tanned, swam and ate. We spent all day at that beach, returning to the cottage for lunch when we saw the Block Island Ferry. Sometimes Moms brought peanut butter and jelly sandwiches and Kool Aid to the beach. I had an RCA portable radio so I could listen to Red Sox games after lunch.

Beach Sitting

A deep tan became summer's signature. My brother Peter made the letters L, I, F, E, G, U, A, R, D with white tape and stuck them to his chest, leaving them until they fell off. In a few days, the words *Life Guard* were "inscribed" in white.

We had no sunscreens, so the first few days of baking were brutal; terrible tender burns, taut skin and gunks of Noxzema Cream at night. We wore an undershirt the next day, even in the water. One day I met a woman from our neighborhood. She looked at me and said I had a great tan, suggesting that it was my Italian blood. I paused. Her white skin was loaded with freckles and was burning.

Days were perfect. It did not rain often, but when it did, we went to the Casino Movie Theater in Narragansett, kids packed in like sardines. The noise blunted the fun of the movie.

The Beach Cabin

At day's end, as the sun dipped into the water, we showered outdoors. What was it about that shower that made us feel so good? It was ice-cold. We were hot and covered with a thin layer of grisly salt and sweat. We were naked, enclosed and protected under the blue sky and fleecy clouds. The cold water was invigorating. The Ivory soap's smell readied us for the Johnson's Baby Powder and the soft, white sweat shirt that smelled, yep, of Ivory Soap.

Nights were nearly as much fun as the days. At sunset we flew kites or walked to the rocks and caught crabs at low tide. On some walks, we took jars for catching fireflies blinking on and off like sparks as they floated away.

On some Saturdays, our Dads crossed to the beach, dug a hole in the ground, threw in rocks and lit a fire where we cooked marshmallows under the stars.

At day's end, with crickets chirping and fireflies flickering, I headed for bed, thoughts of a new day swirling in my head.

Crabbin'

I stared up at the blue, cloudless sky. The beach glistened in the light of the setting sun as it gave way to an early moon. My skin was tight and tender at the back of my neck, and the salted hair on my arms bristled under the rub of my sweatshirt.

The heat of the summer day turned to a cooler evening and thoughts of crabbin'. Friends gathered and, carrying pails, off we trekked to the far end of the beach.

We started our walk behind the lifeguard chair that stood between Cronin's and Dodsworth's Beaches. Jack-the-lifeguard perched there on those long summer days. With a rare move, he came down and strolled the beach. But he was gone for the day.

The variety store with its red shingled roof as our beacon was behind us. People strolled the beach. Others lay on blankets, fixed by the view and the sound of the waves, books by their sides.

Our cabin was a good distance from the curve at beach's end. We walked to the rhythmic sound of rumbling waves dropping their foam on the shore. I swung my red pail with the white handle and leaned forward into the gentle evening wind, a wind that on other evenings took my kite to those distant rocks. The soft sand yielded to mud; the mud gave way to the sudsy water. The smell of seaweed was in the air.

Rocks of all sizes in shades of black, gray, green and brown were littered with seaweed, fishhooks, a network of frayed fishing lines, moss and periwinkles perched like rows of dunce caps.

On the horizon, we spotted the Block Island Ferry. Seagulls skimmed alongside. Ahead of us and beyond the rocks was a mansion on a bluff. I loved that house; a sprawling single-story, yellow home with a black-shingled roof and white gutters. Nearby, anchored by a curved, narrow path bordered by high grass that bent lazily in the soft breezes, was the generous guest house. Another path wound its way from that house to the rocks.

I wondered if rich people crabbed.

The waves broke over the rocks with increasing force. No need to go out too far as our catch would be easy at low tide. The damp air was cool on my face. Slippery, sloping rocks of all sizes, some as big as a couch, were covered with brown seaweed and green moss. There was a bone yard of mussel shells, petrified snails and periwinkles. There were starfish. A snail drew back into his shell. A slip. Now my sneaker was soaked.

I sat on a flat rock, pretending I was in a movie with the tide lapping and swirling among the rocks, mist in my face and the big yellow house behind me. At the distant breaking waves were men in tall boots casting their lines from lofty poles.

Now for bait. A fish head would have been ideal, but a crushed mussel tied to a string would do just fine. I pulled a large, tenacious one from its bed, smashed it with a rock and tied a string around it. I looked at Carol. She needed help. I handed her the end of the string which she held with two fingers and her thumb.

I threw seaweed into the pail, dipped my mussel into the water and waited. The first crab inched out from under the rock. Back he went. Patience. Dangle the bait. Out and back he went. Out again. He paused, grabbed the mussel with his claws and dipped his head into the flesh. I pulled slowly. He was on. I jiggled the crab over the pail, and he fell to the bottom.

Bunches more came. I loaded the pail and watched them crawl, one over the other, some along the smooth sides, undaunted no matter how many times they slipped back. As the sun set in the distance, it was time to go. Balancing pails, we skated over the rocks to the shore, the store in the distance. As I looked back, the rocks disappeared under a thin veil of dusk. The waves glided up and washed my footsteps away.

I showed the catch to Dad. "What are you going to do with them?"

"Keep them."

"And then what?"

"I don't know. Just have them, I guess."

"They'll die, you know. They need to be in the ocean. It might not be a bad idea to let them go." We walked to water's edge. I inverted the pail and dumped the crabs. With claws held high, they scurried into the sea, eventually, I suppose, finding their way to the rocks.

The night sky was violet and gold. I rubbed pieces of beach glass in my pocket. It was time for an ice cream or a frozen Charleston Chew. A soft breeze carried the odor of seaweed. Summers were not long enough.

We See Gorgeous George

On some evenings during our month at the shore, we went to Narragansett Pier, a small village along the water with a movie theater, a lighthouse, an ice cream parlor, a wall and sometimes a band concert at The Casino. The original Casino, one that hosted special events for the wealthy, was battered by the hurricane of '38 and a fire in 1956 and was long gone. One day, I overheard Dad say to Uncle Carlo that Gorgeous George would be 'rasslin' at the rebuilt Casino on Saturday night.

Uncle Carlo said he saw him wrestle at The Arena and thought it might be something special for the boys to see. Gorgeous George was an undefeated world champion known as 'pretty boy' because of his blond curly hair. After dinner, we were off in Uncle Carlo's Packard. I fidgeted as we drove the road along the shore.

The Casino was a circular building with brown wooden shingles and a green roof. It sat in the center of a small park across the street from the wall that buttressed the ocean.

There once had been a tennis court, a bandstand, ballroom dancing and a train station at the site.

The Casino was not what I thought. I had been to boxing matches with Dad and uncle at the Arena in Providence, so I expected it to be the same. Not so. It was clean. The seats were arranged in neat rows. Few were smoking. We had a clear view of the ring and sat below it, looking up at the wrestlers instead of in a smoky arena looking down.

The announcer, dressed in a tuxedo, barked, "Ladees and Junlemen, Ba-fore the main bout … it woonnn't be long … hang on kids … we have some spe-shal contests.…"

The matches took forever; bunches of wrestlers grunting, groaning, toppling, beads of sweat flying, shoes squeaking … up, down, up, down … Who cared? Finally, the main event.

Now, the announcer's voice rose to a metallic shrill … "La-dees 'n Junlemen." I leaned forward, spilling some popcorn. "The main event of the evening … one of the world's greatest wrestlers, un–de–feat–ed heavyweight champeen … " on he droned. Hurry up, willya! Let's see him. And there, there he was!

The crowd stood as George sauntered along the short aisle and entered the ring, ducking through the ropes and strutting to all four corners like a peacock. He had curly, long blond hair and wore a large purple flowing robe and a feathered cape with sequins. Just the tips of his white boots showed. He hardly looked like the other 'rasslas' we had just seen. Uh oh. Was he throwing roses? He was! He was throwing roses while bouncing on his toes from one foot to the other!

Screams of "Sissy, Sissss ... y," came from the dark areas in the rear of the converted dance floor. George smiled and chuckled ... "Heh, heh, heh ... " like a villain. There was more.

He threw gold-plated bobby pins to the crowd. They picked them up and threw them back. George made a spin, flared his cape and took it off in one smooth move. He removed his boots and was now down to bare feet and leather shorts that looked like the ones Tarzan wore, slits along the side.

His opponent, absent an entourage, wore black shorts, high black shoes and no robe. He seemed bored with the show and stood in his corner flat footed with his arms curled backwards over the ropes. The crowd alternated jeering with chanting ... Booo, booo, Gor-jous, Gor-jus, Gor-jus ...bing, bing, bing, bing, the bell. The gladiators jumped to their toes and walked to the middle of the ring. George's opponent stuck out his hand. George turned his back. His bored challenger shrugged. In a flash, they whirled around and grabbed shoulders and necks.

George's opponent was now on the attack, looking good, doing everything but killing George with slams, punches, spins and throws. Once, George landed out of the ring near us. He arose slowly, pulled his shorts down and crept back into the ring to a scrunch of the other guy's shoe on his back. "He's done," I thought, but I was close enough to realize that the shoe slam was soft, barely touching George even though he winced when his chest hit the mat.

"Dad, IS HE FAKING?"

"You bet," said Dad. "You bet," said Uncle Carlo. In unison, they proclaimed, "This guy's a phony! You phony." Dad and Uncle were into it. Then came the final pick-um-up-above-the-head slam. Gorgeous was flattened like a pancake.

He looked dead, lying prone, feet crossed and about to be twisted into the mat. Suddenly, energized and rising from the depths, Gorgeous staggered and in an instant flipped his leg, his foot catching the opponent just under the chin. Thwap! His knees buckled like cooked spaghetti. Bang! George took over with leg drops that caved in rib cages, swirls that made us dizzy and a final slam after lifting his opponent high over his head and twirling him helicopter style. As the guy lay prone on the deck, George straddled him and did the despicable, the dirtiest stunt of all. He took a gold bobby pin from his hair and turning out of view of the ref, who always seemed in the wrong position, picked up the guy's head by the hair and began to gouge out his eye.

We screamed, "Ref, ref, look, look, he has a bobby pin in that guy's eye! He has a bobby pin! Look! Look!" George turned and the ref, collected in his white shirt, bow tie and creased black pants was on the wrong side, again. He made a quick move to look, but George put the pin back in his hair. "It's in his hair. It's in his hair." But the ref paid no attention.

"Dad, he did that on purpose. This is a joke. Everybody is faking, even the ref."

"Yes, Edward. You don't think that George had a bobby pin in the guy's eye, do you?"

The bout was over, the opponent near dead and slumped in a corner, George the winner, standing on his toes, the ref holding his hand high to the lights above. What a show.

How did Gorgeous George happen to come to this little casino here in Narragansett?

Dad thought there were lots of Gorgeous George look-alikes who travelled the country. I was surprised and a little disappointed. Then Dad told me that the Georges wrestled the same guys every night in every town. Oh dear.

It was late. I was tired. But what a night. Gorgeous George was *phenomenal.*

Summer Movies, Charleston Chews, Citronella and Mosquitoes

Among the many things we did during those summers was to go to an outdoor movie on a Saturday night. What could be better than a show at the seashore in the summer, waves crashing in the distance, stars, salt air, moon and mist?

Adams, the general store less than a mile away, presented the movies. Though exhausted after a day at the beach, we became invigorated when the sun was setting and the thought of the movies crept to the fore. Before leaving, we received our orders:

"Take a blanket. It will get cold when that sun goes down."

After baking all day, I replied, "Cold? Mom, I'm boiling hot. I don't need a blanket? I'm wearing my sweatshirt and khaki pants. I'll be fine. I'll look stupid carrying a blanket."

"OK. Have it your way."

"Take the Citronella for the mosquitoes," said Aunt Della. "It will keep them away. They will eat you alive."

"Citronella? What's that?"

"Take it. Take it. Rub it all over. Even in your hair."

I lost that battle, so I stuffed the bottle into my back pocket.

"And take this flashlight. You'll need it when you walk home." She handed me Uncle Carlo's flashlight. Now this was different. It was an olive-colored Army flashlight with the light at right angles to the handle. I clipped it to my belt.

We were off, walking alongside a marsh awash with wild roses, tall grasses, pussy willows, cat-o-nine-tails and acrobatic swallows. The crickets were busy. Lightning bugs consorted with us. Excitement built as the sun disappeared over the beach and the field across the street.

Set in the store's lot was a wooden screen painted white and attached to a four-foot post. Above the screen was a gray, cone-shaped speaker. (On those long, dreary winter Sundays when we needed a change and rode to the beach, I spotted the screen. It was sturdy in the barren lot as it awaited summer).

A low wall separating the theater from the store was a place to sit, though we usually sat on the grass. Behind the wall and propped on a tall table was a projector with two reels. A black wire ran from the projector along the back of the lot to and through a barely open store window. Toward the rear of the lot, the adults sat on beach chairs.

A murmur of anticipation welled up. The kids now started to whistle and chant, "Moo-vie, Moo-vie, Moo-vie." The projectionist told us to be patient. I went for a Charleston Chew.

The sun set behind a haze over the beach. The surf tumbled in the distance.

Suddenly, rows of speeding white spots flashed up on the screen. The crowd cheered when the Bugs Bunny cartoon came on.

The soft lights bathing the parking lot and the one streaming from the projector attracted swarms of moths, an army of gnats and an occasional plump June bug that droned and swerved in like a B52. An annoying, whining buzz … zzzz, bzzzz, izzzz … tickled my ears. I felt a nip on my hand. I slapped. Splat. Flattened. Blood! Mosquitoes! Platoons of them arose from the nearby marsh. They swarmed like enemy bombers, attacking feverishly, sparing no bare skin. The mob of movie watchers waved, squirmed and slapped in the dance of the evening.

I pulled my sweatshirt over my hands. They attacked my neck. I scrunched my nose under the collar. They attacked my face, my ears and my ankles. It was time for that stuff Aunt Della gave me. I whipped the bottle from my rear pocket. The label read, "Citronella Oil. Hours of protection."

I spread the pale yellow oil on my face (ugh) neck, hands and ankles, but not in my hair. No way. The stink of oil and lemon was sickening, but not for the mosquitoes. They loved it … slurp, ummm, bzzz, ummm, izzzz … tickle, slurp, sting. They dove to dine. Slap … wave … swat … slam … welt … oil … nothing helped. "Hey, are any of you guys getting bit? Or is it just me? Dammit. This is awful. They should have sprayed the marsh with DDT!"

A cool breeze from the ocean swept the bugs away for a moment, but it met the steam curling up from the land and brought a cool, damp mist that crept across the gravel, smothered the screen with a milky glow and made the light from the projector monster-like eerie. A distant horn blew over the water. A passing car purred, its barely visible taillights engulfed by the mist. I smelled the ocean's salt and felt its dew land softly on my face. The grass where we sat was damp.

My sun-warmed skin was cold; shivers preceded goose bumps that spread like poison ivy. I rolled down the cuffs of my khakis and snuck my chin and nose further into my soap-scented sweatshirt. I wished I had a blanket. I had to pee. Covered with goose bumps blended with bites, now I kinda wanted to be in my warm bed in the cabin. Wait. More white spots sped across the screen and replaced the movie with nothing but a chalky shine.

"Boo, hiss," The crowd was restless, tired, cold and eaten.

"Hang on, hang on, kids. Gimme a break willya. Gimmee a break!" pleaded the projectionist. "The film didn't snap. The movie just slipped off the sprocket." A what? "I'll get it fixed. Hold your horses." It was an opportune moment for me to sneak behind the wall to pee in the bushes. Post pee shivers accompanied the misty cold. I ducked into the store. It smelled of popcorn, chocolate, food, wood and warmth.

The projectionist prevailed. Finally, thankfully, "The End." The crowd clapped. Two small floodlights came on. Folding chairs snapped. Car engines started. The fog lifted. The horn stopped. It was time to go home.

What a night! Goose bumps, bites, blood, cold, shivers and all, it was worth every moment. As we started our walk back accompanied by fireflies under a clear sky with a full moon, brilliant stars and crashing waves, I whipped the flashlight off my belt, flipped it on and handed it to cousin Bill. "Let's go. Show us the way, Bill."

I was so lucky to spend a night away from the hot city with friends and family at the beach and with a movie. It meant summer. I never took it for granted.

A Nightmare at the Beach

When I was ten, our families visited Lido Beach most Sundays. This day would be different however. I was excited to think that I might stay at the beach in an Army tent with three older friends. What could be a problem for just one night? Well, it became a nightmare.

Ted, my neighborhood friend in the city, said it would be a great experience; a real Army tent. And we were assured of a ride home in the morning.

In a tent. A night away from home. No radio. No parents. No prepared breakfast. What if we didn't get the ride? Providence was miles away. It gave me pause. Ted assured my parents that I would be OK, that we had a ride and that he would keep a close eye on me. Mom looked at Dad. They agreed with hesitation. Dad turned to Mom, then me and said something like, "Edward, are you sure you are OK with this? It gets very dark here. And cold. And damp."

"Edward," Mom chimed, "Remember the night you came home from Wally's tent at nine o'clock because you were scared?"

"Yes, Mom. I was seven. There were noises."

Dad asked the lifeguard, our driver, if the morning ride was definite. He was reassured. As an added precaution, he gave me ten dollars for any emergency. I looked around and stuffed it in my pocket.

They got in the car and Dad started the engine. I walked toward the tent, turned and stood on my toes to watch the back of Dad's Chevy turn out of the lot, the L49 number plate barely visible. I slumped. Ted put his arm around my shoulder. He knew I was frightened and already homesick. He led me to my cot at the back of the tent where I sat, hunched over and let out a little sob. After a walk to the beach, it was dark and time for bed. Back to the cot.

I took my sneakers off and tucked the $10 in one of them. I huddled under the musty blanket, lay on my side and used my towel for a pillow. The lantern brought dancing shadows and outlines of others, two of whom were strangers, slipping into their cozy sleeping bags. Shivering, I scrunched under my blanket to rebreathe my warm air as the mist and the cold rolled in. Wind shook the flaps. The roof waffled. I was cold, homesick and frightened.

Voices in the distance comforted me, but soon they were gone. So was the hum of cars. The moon's light helped a little. I recited the Red Sox lineup … DiMaggio, Goodman, Pesky, Vern Stephens Williams … to myself and finally fell asleep. The night passed. I woke to early morning stirring. The guys were up. I sat up, looked around and stuck my hand in my sneaker. The ten dollars was gone. I checked the other. Not there either. The money was gone! Could someone have stolen it? I told Ted.

"Really. Are you sure you didn't drop it? Who could've taken it?"

"I don't think I dropped it. I put it in my sneaker" The guys I didn't know were gone. I looked at my watch, eager to know when we were leaving. Ted said around ten. He went to check with the lifeguard. The rising sun met its twin on the water. Paths of orange penetrated the fleecy clouds. It would be another steamy summer day.

Ted returned with his head hung low and a puzzled frown. "Bad news. The lifeguard ain't goin' to the city, so we can't get a ride from him. But there's a guy goin' to Cranston and we can thumb a ride from there." I was hungry.

After what seemed an eternity, we left at noon. It was hot. We got into a Studebaker with rear windows that did not open; four of us crowded into the small space. I was squashed against the unopened window. Whatever breeze there was blew hot.

It took forever to get to Cranston. We stopped near the Brewery. I squeezed out of the car . It was hotter. I was thirsty, hungry, broke and miles from home yet.

I tagged along with my bathing suit wrapped in my towel and slung over my shoulder. We thumbed. Car after car passed. We walked with dead legs on steaming streets. My socks crept under my heels and my feet were scorched. Rivulets of sweat rolled alongside my ears. Beads collected on my lip. The smell of salt water was long gone, but not the feel. My tee-shirt stuck to the few hairs I had, scratching across them with each step. I wanted to be in a tub of water with Ivory Soap. I wanted to be home.

I remember little more save for walking by the hospital now only a few blocks from home. My aunt Della was a patient, having just delivered her son Steven. She was sitting with my grandmother when, as she looked out the window, she spotted me. "Ma, that's Edward. That's Edward. Look, down there. It's him. I'm sure. He's walking."

Finally, late afternoon, my street. Familiar, comfortable sidewalks and houses . Mom met me at the door. "Edward, what happened? You're sweating and red. You look so hot. What happened?" I climbed the three flights with barely enough energy to speak.

"We had to walk home from the beach. Someone stole my money."

"I knew it. Stole your money?" I walked to the bathroom sink, doused my head with cold water and let it run over my hands and arms. Mom made me a baloney sandwich with the best Kool Aid ever.

"I told your father it was not a good idea to let you stay there alone. You walked from Narragansett?"

"Not quite. From Cranston. Mom, I was with the guys."

"Never mind." She said that a lot.

It was so good to be home. That night, after a bath, I crawled into my cool bed, covered myself with the cool, clean sheet and turned on the radio. There were soft lights coming from the kitchen and the moon. I went to sleep with no lineup in my head.

Aunt Della told the story for years. "I was in my hospital room and saw Edward walk by in that hot sun."

What a lesson. As days and years passed, it seemed like it was easier to now affirm that I was a hero for what I did. The story of my bravery grew.

I slept in a tent with the guys at the beach.

I lost my money.

I walked for miles in the heat.

I grew up.

She Passes By

In the summer of 1952, when I was thirteen and staying at the beach house, something stirred in me that I had not experienced. After supper, we usually played softball in the small, grassy field facing the cabins across the street from the beach.

One evening, ambling by and silhouetted against the sinking sun, was a girl with blond hair tied in a ponytail. I shielded my eyes. Her white sweatshirt accentuated her tan. She turned, smiled, raised her hand and scrunched a little wave. I looked around. She was waving at me!

I crouched down, rose to my toes, stood straight up, brushed my sweatshirt and started a slow walk. My heart was racing. I stopped, stuffed my shirt in, tightened my belt and scratched the back of my calf with the top of my sneaker. I restarted, picking up the pace, near skipping.

I think she was older. She was tall and very pretty. As she turned her head, her ponytail blew in the breeze. Her eyes were soft and sparkly.

Her smile was wide.

I took a breath, took my hat off and ran my hand over the stubble of my rah-rah.

I tapped my glove like Doerr and pawed the dirt like Williams. I wish I had carried my bat. After an inaugural silence, I eked out a "Hi." I was looking for her to run with my opening. She did.

"Hi. I saw you playing." My face reddened through my tan. She fiddled with her gimp bracelet. I had a gimp bracelet.

I searched for words. "Oh, yeah, thanks," being among my better choices. I put my right hand in my pocket. The left still held the glove. She asked my name. I told her Eddie. I should have said Ed. With an urge to return to shortstop, I realized how shy and young I was. I looked into her eyes for a millisecond. I think they were blue.

"I'm Ann (my mother's name). I'm staying with a friend. Maybe I'll see you tomorrow. Or maybe at the outdoor movie on Saturday. You go to the movies, don't you?"

Meet? The outdoor movie. My favorite. "Yes. I love them. I go every Friday at home. With friends. Go to the Creamery for ice cream after. OK, see ya." I was as excited as if I had hit a grand slam. Her hair swung from side to side as she walked away. I ran at top speed back to the game. Uncle Carl smiled as I sped by.

When settled, I watched her in the distance. I forgot to ask where she was staying or where she lived in the city. Tomorrow, maybe.

That night, I lay in bed, thinking. I imagined holding her hand. The next morning, I bounded out of bed, slipped on my bathing suit, skipped breakfast and hustled to the beach. There was no one there. I strolled to the next. Vacant. Too early perhaps. The rest of the week was no different, no matter the time. During the days, I walked the beaches more than usual, but she was not to be found.

On Saturday evening, I sped to the outdoor movie. Ann was not there. I never saw her again. She became a summer memory.

The beach beckoned us by day and captured us by night with its steady, predictable rhythm of rising sun, crashing waves, cool breezes and the moon's reflections. There was more this year, more than just a beach. Something stirred in me for the first time.

Now, as I write this, I realize how goofy I was and for how long that lasted. When I think of those summer days, I also realize how lucky I was.

At July's end, it was time to return to the city. One evening, I sat on a rock and looked at the ocean, the crimson sky and the setting sun. Save for the crackling waves, everything was silent. The infinite rhythm of the ocean was like the ticking metronome in music class. It wasn't the melancholy-last-days-of-summer ticking. It was the melancholy ticking of the last days of *summer at the beach*. I still had August.

It felt good. I felt good. It had to be good. I was suspended in time. Can it be that it will only and ever be the summer that I was thirteen?

Those days at the beach filled me with joy, molding the early days of youth, the memory of a fleeting moment adding even more. From that moment, things started to change. I began to realize what was happening.

EPILOGUE

That's it. This takes me to my early teens.

Though these stories may seem a bit storybook and repetitious, nevertheless, they are as I lived and remember them. My life seems to have unfolded in snippets. Writing helps me keep a hold on them.

Of course, there is repetition, but when one writes in bursts of thought and with short essays, there almost has to be. Perhaps they should not be read in one sitting but rather one at a time, maybe every other day.

It doesn't matter. This is how I remember them. This is how I want to share them.

This is my legacy; the dynamics of my early youth … who I am and how I was made.

Putnam Street School is gone. Academy Avenue School is gone, both due to the condo craze and the integration of schools. George West is now a middle school. The ballfields are small. Streets are different. Neighborhoods change. They have to. I have.

The past may sometimes be blurry, but what I wrote is what I remember.

The writing helps me keep a hold on things that I cherish while filling me with joy and satisfaction.

Thank you for reading.

You can order all of Dr. Ed's books and subscribe to his blog at:

www.edwrites.com

Made in the USA
Middletown, DE
16 June 2021